Gladys Aylward

by
Fern Neal Stocker

A Guessing Book

MOODY PRESS
CHICAGO

© 1988 by
THE MOODY BIBLE INSTITUTE
OF CHICAGO

All Scripture quotations are from the King James Version.

Illustrations are by Virginia Hughins.

Library of Congress Cataloging in Publication Data

Stocker, Fern Neal, 1917-
    Gladys Aylward / by Fern Neal Stocker.
        p.   cm. — (A Guessing book)
    Summary: Recounts the life of the uneducated, visually handicapped British woman who served as a missionary in China for many years, setting up orphanages to help homeless children. At intervals in the text the reader finds a question followed by several possible answers, one or more of which may be correct.
    ISBN 0-8024-3047-3
    1. Aylward, Gladys—Juvenile literature.   2. Missionaries—China--Biography—Juvenile literature.   3. Missionaries—England--Biography—Juvenile literature.   [1. Aylward, Gladys.
2. Missionaries.   3. Literary recreations.]   I. Title.   II. Series:
Stocker, Fern Neal, 1917-   Guessing book.
BV3427.A9S76   1988
266'.0092'4—dc19
[B]
[92]   88-23026
                                                                             CIP
                                                                             AC

1 2 3 4 5 6 7 Printing/LC/Year 92 91 90 89 88

Printed in the United States of America

To my daughter—Elizabeth Long

Contents

To You, the Reader:

A Guessing Book is the story of a famous person. As you read along in this Guessing Book, you'll come to questions you can answer by yourself.

One, two, or three guesses are given, and you can choose one, two, or three answers. Sometimes all are correct, sometimes none. (You'll find the answer as you keep reading.) Pretty soon you'll know the person in the story so well you can get the answer right every time.

It may be fun to keep track of how many guesses you get right. But if you miss one, don't worry—this isn't a test.

Read this Guessing Book and learn about Gladys Aylward, a woman who was bold and brave for God.

1

Dumb Eyes

"Gladys Ayl-ward is so dumb.
"Gladys Ayl-ward is so dumb."

The singsong tone of half the fifth-grade class taunted Gladys. Three girls and four boys circled her at recess time. This was not her first teasing, but this time Gladys did not howl or scream in rage. She

GUESS

1. cried.
2. bowed her head.
3. told the teacher.

When Gladys raised her bowed head, she said softly, "I know. I know I'm dumb."

Her classmates stared at her. "How unlike Gladys!" one said. Then slowly they moved to other parts of the playground. "She's no fun that way," Mary said, kicking a stone.

"I thought she'd holler like she did before, crazy-like." Frances looked over her shoulder to see Gladys walk toward the schoolhouse.

Before the door Gladys stopped. She thought, *I can't read*

GUESS

1. *blackboards.*
2. *signs.*
3. *books.*

I wonder why I can't read books, when I can read the blackboard.

Looking around the school yard, hedged with bushes, Gladys reminded herself, *I'd be out there jumping rope and playing right now except for Miss Primsley. Why, oh, why did she make me read? She knows I can't read, and everyone hates to wait. If only I could read like the others. If only I weren't so dumb. If only . . .*

Miss Primsley came out and rang a little bell. Students

GUESS

1. lined up behind Gladys.
2. marched inside.
3. screamed and yelled.

As Gladys led the line of students to their seats, she noticed they were quiet.

Before Miss Primsley came into the classroom, Mary said, "We are sorry we teased you, Gladys. We only do it because you are so funny. But we won't anymore, will we?" Mary cast a hard glance at her classmates, who nodded shamefacedly.

"After all, I guess you can't help it if you are dumb," Frances added. Then she clapped her hands over her mouth. Everyone started to laugh. Frances quickly added, "Since Miss Primsley hasn't come yet, why don't you mimic her?"

Gladys turned around and stared into friendly faces. The sea of eyes looked ashamed, and Gladys

GUESS

1. felt better.
2. stood up.
3. made a face.

12

Slowly Gladys stood up. Since she felt better, she began imitating the teacher.

Waddling to the blackboard like Miss Primsley, she picked up a wooden pointer. Rapping the board she mimicked Miss Primsley's voice. "Now, young ladies and gentlemen, look here." The class roared, and Gladys was off, swaying, nodding, and pursing her lips like her teacher.

But Gladys didn't know Miss Primsley was

GUESS	1. sick.
	2. hurt.
	3. listening.

Miss Primsley listened in the hallway.

Gladys went on and on. The more the pupils laughed, the greater effort she made.

Finally Miss Primsley walked in. Pursing her lips, she said,

GUESS	1. "That is enough."
	2. "Very good, Gladys."
	3. "Go to the principal's office."

Everyone froze when she said, "Very good, Gladys. Can you imitate anyone else?"

Gladys gazed at her. She didn't answer until she was sure Miss Primsley was genuinely amused.

"Well, uh, sometimes I do the Chinese laundryman," Gladys ventured.

"Go ahead. Do it!"

Since Gladys often practiced at home, she began to perform. When Miss Primsley sat down and laughed with the class, Gladys continued in her best Chinese tones. She frantically waved her arms, asked questions, and finally screamed, "No tickee, no washee."

Miss Primsley wiped her eyes. "Gladys, you are a wonderful mimic, but, my dear, you will never get anywhere in life if you can't do your schoolwork. Please try harder. Promise me!"

13

Gladys's shoulders slumped. She nodded miserably as she took her seat. She thought, *I do try hard!*

All afternoon Gladys waited. Miss Primsley finally said, "Turn! Stand! Pass!" As the pupils marched past the teacher's desk, she returned papers to them from the previous day.

"What did you get?" the pupils asked each other. But no one asked Gladys, for she

GUESS	1. started hitting everyone.
	2. raced home alone.
	3. hid.

Since Gladys knew no one could catch her, she ran toward home. With skirts flying above gray stockings and stout shoes, she raced past rows of brick houses with lace curtains. Red geraniums nodded to her from every window.

When she reached Cheddington Road, she stopped and looked at her grades. "F" on every paper. "Mum will beat me," she wailed, wishing Mum *would* beat her instead of looking so sad.

When Gladys banged the back door, Mum called,

GUESS	1. "Careful with that door."
	2. "Hang up your coat."
	3. "Come have tea with me."

Gladys knew this was their time to talk. Today, however, her feet dragged as she joined her mother in the west room for tea.

The late afternoon sun streamed through white lace curtains. Gladys looked at her mother in a wicker chair before the tea table. *If only I could be pretty like Mum.* Gladys sighed as she sat down, carefully hiding her papers.

"How was school today?" Mum asked as she filled Gladys's cup.

Through stiff lips Gladys told the story—the terrible reading, the teasing, the mimicking, and the "F" papers. The sobs came at last.

"My dear, I've given a great deal of thought to your problem. Do you want to know what I think?" Mum asked.

"Yes." Gladys looked up hopefully. "You know I try as hard as I can."

Mum rose and pulled Gladys to her feet. Putting her arms around her, she said, "You do, and don't forget God made you the way you are *for a reason*. I don't know what the reason is—and you don't—but *He* knows. There is something you can do, something no one else in the world can do. Someday you will know what it is. In the meantime, what would you like to be?"

"I'd like to be

GUESS	1. an actress." 2. a missionary." 3. a nursemaid."

Gladys brightened. "I'd like to be an actress." Then seeing her mother's look, she added, "Or a missionary."

"Well, we shall see." Mum looked serious. "You'd need schooling for either one."

As the two sat down again, they heard the clomping of Father's postman boots on the front steps.

"Cheerio," they called. Just then three younger children burst through the back door.

Gladys and her mother watched as Father picked up each child. When the noisy greetings were over, he sent Violet and the twin brothers to the kitchen.

Turning to Mum, he asked, "And why so sober?" She told him Gladys's story as she gave him a cup of tea.

"I've been afraid of this, Gladys," he said sternly. "There is no use wasting any more money on your schooling. Besides, everyone in London is talking about

GUESS	1. war." 2. peace." 3. fun."

15

"War, war, war. That's all I hear," Father said.

"But how does that affect Gladys?" Mum asked.

"War affects us all—you'll see. Gladys can help by caring for the younger children. Violet, of course, can stay in school, and you, my dear wife, can help at the hospital. It's going to take everyone in England to lick the Kaiser, wicked man that he is. Yes, we need everyone—even Gladys with her dumb eyes."

"My dumb eyes?" Gladys questioned.

"Of course." Father smiled. "There's nothing dumb about *you*. I don't know how bad eyes can help in this war, but we'll soon find out."

2
War

After two years of war, the Aylward family gathered together in the west room. Father, dressed in his dark postman's uniform, spoke seriously. "Remember, Gladys is in charge when we are at work. She is fourteen now, and I'm holding her responsible. You do as she says." Father glared at the younger children. "Now I want to tell you how to protect yourself if the bombings reach us." Gladys saw him lift his chin, and she heard the fear in his voice. She knew if the bombs hit their house

GUESS

1. everyone would be killed.
2. the house would cave in.
3. only God could save them.

"See this wall?" Father pointed. "It is the strongest in our house. If the zeppelins come with their bombs, sit on the floor beside this wall. And pray," he added, "for only God can save you!"

Gladys tore her frightened gaze from her father long enough to note Mum's pale face and Violet's eyes dark with fear.

"Come inside where you will be safe."

She saw the twins cling together on one stool. She heard Baby Laurie whining as he crawled on the floor. Gladys pulled the baby into her lap and began to hum softly as Father continued. After two years of caring for the younger children, Gladys was

GUESS

1. bossy.
2. mean.
3. loving.

Love filled Gladys's heart. That could not be crowded out by fear. *I'll protect them some way,* she told herself.

When Father and Mother were at work six days later, the test came.

"I see the balloons! I see them!" Violet screamed as she ran into the house.

In an instant Gladys was outside gazing into the sky. One, two, three zeppelins she counted. "They look like fat sausages. Who would think they carry bombs?"

The twins flew around the corner and clutched at Gladys's skirts. "Will they bomb us? Will they? Will they?"

"Not today," Gladys said, hoping she spoke the truth. "But run quick! Sit with your back against the wall, draw up your knees and bow your heads, like Father said."

She was about to go inside when she noticed neighborhood children running wildly in the street. "Don't be afraid," she called. "Come here!"

Nine or ten children

GUESS

1. came to her.
2. made faces.
3. ran away.

"Come in. My father told us what to do. Come inside where you will be safe."

As the children came, Gladys noticed the wild looks fade from their eyes. "Go inside. See how the children sit with legs folded. Sit with them," she urged.

Once the group settled, Gladys went outside and gathered more frantic, screaming children, who were running this way and that in a frenzy. "Come inside, sit quietly, pray," she directed.

The house creaked under the weight of children. When the first bombs hit London, Gladys shut the door, but the noise shook the room. Children

GUESS	1. whined.
	2. trembled.
	3. sang.

Everyone sang:

> "Tramp, tramp, tramp,
> The boys are marching. . . ."

"Come," Gladys said, "sing so the men in the zeppelins will hear!"

At that the children screamed so loud that

GUESS	1. the Germans heard.
	2. the parents heard.
	3. only God heard.

The crashing of falling buildings, the cries of the wounded, and the crackling of fire drowned the children's voices. Only God heard their shouts.

As the noise of the bombing moved into the distance, the children sat quietly, nursing raw throats. Gladys played hymns softly until someone called out, "I wonder if my house is still standing."

At that everyone stampeded outside. Gladys called to her family, "Stay with me!" Together they gaped at the wrecked buildings.

They saw people beating out fires and frantically pawing in the rubble.

"Oh, I see Father and Mum!" Violet screamed, as their parents forced their way through the crowds and rubble.

"Well done, Gladys," Father said, as he took Baby Laurie from her arms.

3

Parlor Maid

After the war Gladys found the only job open to her,

GUESS
1. a parlor maid.
2. an actress.
3. a circus performer.

Young men, home from the war, took most jobs. Gladys became a parlor maid.

"So *this* is the great thing God has for me!" Gladys laughed to herself.

Always the mimic, Gladys somewhat enjoyed copying her employer's manners. "Do it like this," Mrs. Paddington said. "And say this," she would add.

Gladys said and did each task *exactly* like Mrs. Paddington.

At home, Mum cautioned Gladys, "Be careful, or Mrs. Paddington will think you are making fun of her."

Gladys worked

| GUESS |

1. a year.
2. ten years.
3. two months.

Gladys worked for more than a year at the Paddingtons' before something changed her life.

On Tuesdays, her day off, Gladys usually wandered around downtown London. She examined the theaters and lights. She stared at gentlemen in long coattails and ladies decked out in jewels. She listened for orchestra music coming from open doors of hotels and restaurants.

On this day, however, Gladys turned to the poorer section of London.

There she saw

| GUESS |

1. ragged children.
2. tramps sleeping.
3. painted women.

She saw ragged children, news vendors, and policemen.

Oh, it's all so interesting, she thought.

Later that evening she noticed a group of young people laughing and chatting outside a church. "Come attend the revival meeting," they urged.

The young people

| GUESS |

1. linked their arms in hers.
2. pulled her inside.
3. made jokes.

When two girls linked their arms in hers, Gladys

GUESS

1. agreed.
2. refused.
3. pushed them.

Gladys went along half laughing and half protesting. But when the preacher began, she was annoyed at his words. "God is alive and knows what you are thinking. He loves you and one day will ask for an account of your days and nights."

After the service one of the girls introduced herself. "I'm Olive."

Gladys gave her name and bolted toward the door. The crowd pressed against her, and Olive soon caught up.

"Miss Aylward," Olive coaxed, "I believe God is wanting you!'

"No fear," Gladys answered, "I don't want Him."

Once outside, Gladys ran as fast as she could. The rule at the Paddingtons' was that she be in by ten o'clock, not one minute late.

All week Gladys was uneasy, miserable. *I never should have said I don't want God,* she thought as she tossed in her bed, unable to sleep. *God helped us in the war—Mum said He did. But what could He ever want with me?*

By the following Tuesday, Gladys had a plan. She returned to the church. *Nobody here today,* she thought, and started to go back when she saw

GUESS

1. a store.
2. a sign.
3. an angel.

Gladys saw a sign in front of the house next to the church, "Reverend F. W. Pitt."

Before she could change her mind, she marched to the door and lifted the clapper. A smiling young woman answered the door.

"I'd like to see Reverend Pitt," Gladys sputtered.

24

"He's out." The woman hesitated before she added, "I'm his wife, Frances. Would you like to come in and talk to me?" She held out her hand, and Mrs. Pitt led her inside, where they settled at a table in front of a window.

"Now, my dear, tell me about it," the pastor's wife urged.

Gladys told of her hasty words and ended by saying, "I didn't really mean that I don't want God."

"Then you *do* want Him?" Frances asked. Gladys looked around at the shabby room. There was no music, no religious atmosphere, no dim light. Only a preacher's wife, quoting the Bible and saying, "Jesus is alive today. He said, 'I am the way, the truth, and the life: no man cometh unto the Father, but by me.' Jesus wants to come into your life and take you to God."

Gladys stared. Then she turned away, sniffed, wiped her nose, and pressed her lips together.

"You alone can decide," Frances said. "Do you want God or Satan, heaven or hell?"

The house was silent, waiting for Gladys's answer.

I must decide. I must make up my mind! . . . Then do it! Gladys thought.

"I do want Jesus to take me to God, I do!" she said, grasping Frances's hands.

"And He is willing to take you, if you are willing to go." The preacher's wife slipped her arm around Gladys. They knelt together and prayed beside the sofa.

Gladys said, "Here I am, God. I'm willing!" Then she added, "But what would you want with an ignorant parlor maid?"

4

Changes

After eight years of church attendance, Gladys became interested in missions. "If only I could be a missionary," she confided to Frances Pitt after church one Sunday.

Frances

GUESS

1. encouraged her.
2. discouraged her.
3. didn't care.

"You can, my dear, you can," Frances eagerly urged. "I have friends at the China Inland Mission headquarters right here in London. They give their missionaries a year's training before they send them to China."

"But would they take me?" Gladys looked at her friend. "I never was good in school—only got to the fifth, you know."

"I didn't know, but, no difference. The C.I.M. wants 'all rounders,' anyway."

"What do you mean 'all rounders'?" Gladys puzzled.

"They want practical people who can work with their hands, not just pray and preach." Frances paused. "Let me arrange for you to talk with the director, all right?"

"All right," Gladys answered weakly.

The China Inland Mission

GUESS

1. accepted Gladys.
2. rejected Gladys.
3. said maybe.

In no time Gladys found herself enrolled at the C.I.M. training school for three months' probation. "Maybe you can pass," the director said.

"I can't believe I quit my job and am actually here with two dozen missionary candidates for China."

She gazed at the huge map of China on the wall. Red dots showed where C.I.M. missionaries were working already. Gladys drank up the words of returned missionaries. She prayed and sang from the depths of her heart.

In her dormitory room Gladys said to her roommate, "I love the services and the classes here. The teachers inspire me to love China and the Chinese people. But, oh, the reading. I just can't read books, no matter how hard I try—even the Bible!"

"I don't understand. You quote it so well—best in the class, really. You *must* be able to read it!" Mary, Gladys's roommate, looked at her in astonishment.

"Once I hear the words I can repeat what others say. I can read the notes the teacher puts on the blackboard and all the plaques on the walls. But I don't see how people can read such tiny words in books."

"Oh, you'll catch on," Mary urged. "You're sharp as a tack, you are!"

At the end of three months, however, Gladys knew she

GUESS	1. had not caught on. 2. could do it. 3. was not sharp.

When the director called her into the office, Gladys braced herself. She knew all her papers were marked "F."

"We are so sorry you didn't pass your probation," the director said. "There is no point in your continuing your studies. It is a waste of everyone's time and money."

Gladys hid her tears by looking at the flowered carpet.

"But remember, my dear, many people who were rejected by the C.I.M. have gone on to great works. I remember one—Amy Carmichael. She didn't pass our physical for China when she was here years ago. But God is using her in India to this very day."

"But at least she learned your books! It's not your fault I can't learn like Miss Carmichael." Gladys again looked at the floor.

"And what will you do now?"

Gladys gazed into the concerned eyes of the director. She said,

GUESS	1. "I'll be a parlor maid." 2. "I'll go home." 3. "I don't know."

After a long pause, she said, "I don't know."

"There is a way you can help us, Gladys. We have a returning missionary and his wife, who are old and sick. Someone in Bristol has offered a house. But the missionaries arrive next week, and there is no one to care for them." The director hesitated. "Would you take the job?"

Gladys said

GUESS	1. no. 2. yes. 3. maybe.

28

"I—well, I could do it. Guess it's the closest I'll ever get to China. Yes, I'll do it," Gladys decided.

Next day Gladys took her suitcase and boarded a bus on Pentonville Road. She rode past Kings Cross Station to the Marble Arch and changed busses. "Only forty minutes, and I'll be home."

Mum was waiting. "Oh, Gladys, I'm so sorry," she said, as she led her daughter to the west room. "Put your suitcase down, and hang up your coat. Then come have a spot of tea."

Gladys smiled. "You'd tell me to hang up my coat if I were returning from heaven!"

"Now, now, Gladys, come tell me about your plans. Or do you have any?"

"Yes. I'm going to Bristol to care for some old missionaries, so I'll only have two days at home. It's not much of a job—not like going to China, anyway."

"Don't turn up your nose at any job in these hard times. Aren't you afraid of the responsibility?"

"No, but I wish

GUESS	1. I could go to China." 2. it were exciting." 3. the people were young."

Gladys said, "I wish I were going to China instead."

"Be careful what you wish for, Gladys," Mum warned. "God might give it to you."

"I don't see how. I spoiled my chances when I got those 'F' papers at the China Inland Mission. If only I could read the Bible and books like other people." Gladys finished her tea. She shook her head when Mum offered to refill her cup.

"God doesn't expect from people what they're not capable of doing. If He wants you to read, He'll make a way. If He wants you in China, He'll do that, too. But He'll not ask you if you're not able."

"Then why do I feel He's asking when I'm not *able?*"

Mum stared at Gladys. "I don't know, but you have to do the best with what you've got. You go to Bristol and do well. Every time you give up pleasure for duty, you're a stronger person."

So Gladys took a train to Bristol. She didn't know

GUESS

1. her dreams would come true.
2. her life was in danger.
3. the house was haunted.

How could Gladys suspect that staying with two old people could make her dreams come true?

The church people of Bristol amazed Gladys. They had

GUESS

1. the house ready.
2. food in the pantry.
3. forgotten the missionaries.

"Oh, child!" the women exclaimed when they met her train. "You're so small—only five feet, and slender, too."

Gladys had a difficult time turning from one to the other as the women discussed her.

One said, "I like her dark eyes, oval face, and black hair."

Another said, "But she looks stubborn and strong."

"You'll do! I'm Mrs. Stanton." One of the women took her hand. "Don't mind them none. They have to talk about everyone. We got the house ready and food in the pantry."

Somewhat overcome, Gladys followed closely beside Mrs. Stanton, who shooed the crowd away.

At the gate to a solid brown clapboard house, the lady said, "Now, dear, let me show you the place so you can get ready to welcome the missionaries tomorrow. We've arranged a buggy to bring them from the station. We're so excited about having real missionaries with us!"

Gladys listened to Mrs. Stanton's directions. When she was finally alone in her cheerful yellow bedroom, she thought, *I don't even know the names of the missionaries. I wonder if they will be friendly. Was it a mistake to come here?*

5

Bristol

The missionaries were Dr. and Mrs. Fisher. Less than three weeks after they arrived, Gladys knew she had

| GUESS |

1. new friends.
2. problems.
3. enemies.

One warm, sunny day Gladys dashed into the backyard, threw up her arms, and said, "Thank You, thank You, Jesus, for letting me know the Fishers."

She thought of the old couple, he with his white beard and cane and she with her eternal hurrying on tottering legs. "They forget they are in their eighties!"

At the thump, thump, thump of the cane scraping on the hardwood floor, Gladys rushed back into the house and to the front bedroom.

"Yes, Reverend, I'm coming. What can I do for you now?"

"I want to read the Bible. Get it for me, and my glass, too, please."

"I'll get it, Sir, but your wife is making a cake in the kitchen. She can't come to read to you just now."

"I didn't say I wanted her. I said bring my glass. I'm strong enough to sit up now. I'll read it myself, if you'll just fetch my glass."

Gladys placed the Bible on his lap and asked, "Your glass? You mean a glass of water?"

"Mercy, no, girl—don't act stupid. I want that magnifying glass on the dresser."

Gladys hurried to the dresser and picked up a round glass with a long handle. "This?" she asked.

"Yes, girl, be quick!"

"I—I thought it was a mirror," Gladys said, handing it to the missionary. "What's it for?"

Dr. Fisher opened the Bible and held the glass over it. "See?" he said.

Startled, Gladys stepped backward. "The words are jumping off the page. They are big, like—like posters. Oh, Reverend, I can read them, I can!"

"Come closer." The missionary tried to quiet Gladys's prancing. "You mean you could never read the Bible before?"

"No, no, Sir. I always got F on all my papers. Father said it was my dumb eyes."

"Indeed. I marvel no one suggested a magnifying glass and a large print Bible. This is the only way I can read to myself. Why don't you

GUESS	1. use my glass."
	2. read to me."
	3. make a poster."

Dr. Fisher suggested Gladys read to him.
She

GUESS	1. said no.
	2. tried.
	3. failed.

32

At first Gladys needed help with many words, but as the days passed she stumbled less and less. "You try too hard, Gladys. Give yourself time, my dear," Mrs. Fisher suggested.

One day Mrs. Stanton brought some hot rolls. Entering the kitchen, she noticed the young girl. "Land sakes, Gladys! You've got the

GUESS	1. measles." 2. pinkeye." 3. mumps."

"You've got the pinkeye for sure, Gladys. Get out of here. You'll give it to the missionaries. Now, get. Go to Mrs. Warren's. She'll know what to do with you."

Gladys's protests did no good. She soon found herself with her bag packed and directions to Ashley Downs.

To reach Ashley Downs, Gladys trudged through a narrow street and down a long hill. She tramped through the business area. Gladys was impressed by

GUESS	1. wide streets. 2. tall buildings. 3. wild dogs.

The wide streets impressed Gladys, along with the tall brick and stone buildings. Some stood five stories high. *What a pleasant walk this is,* she thought.

But once she turned her corner, she found herself on a narrow street that pointed

GUESS	1. up. 2. down. 3. flat.

33

The street ran up a steep hillside. *Wonder why the houses don't fall off?* she thought. By the time Gladys reached Ashley Downs, she was gasping for breath.

She passed five enormous brick buildings. "I hear children's voices everywhere. What a racket!"

Once Gladys found Mrs. Warren's number, she knocked and explained Mrs. Stanton's orders.

"Settle in, girl, and then let me look at those eyes," Mrs. Warren directed.

After she medicated Gladys's eyes she listened to her questions.

"Ma'am, why did I hear children's voices coming from those buildings I passed?"

"Oh, those are Mueller's orphans. He took them off the streets and gave them a good home. There are more than a thousand there even now."

"Really," Gladys marveled. "He must be very rich."

"No, no, he was a poor man. Been dead thirty years now, but God still supplies the needs of the orphans."

"You mean George Mueller was with a missionary organization, like the C.I.M.?" Gladys pressed.

"No, not at all."

"Then how could he take in orphans, build those five big buildings, buy clothes and food, and—and everything they need?"

"Well, it's like this, Gladys. He took in the orphans and prayed for God to support them. You might say he just had faith."

"That's all?" Gladys gasped.

"That's enough," Mrs. Warren said, "when your faith is in God."

Gladys didn't sleep that night. She

GUESS

1. quoted Bible verses.
2. prayed.
3. sang.

Gladys prayed. "Will You give me faith like George Mueller?" she asked God.

In a few days the red color left her eyes, and Gladys went back to care for the missionaries.

"Dr. Fisher," she said, "now I know my burden for China will be lifted. Either I'll go to China myself, or God will send someone else."

Mrs. Fisher smiled. "God never lets you down! He sends you, guides you, provides for you. He is the One who answers your prayers. You are right to trust Him. I know."

"Yes, Ma'am. Jesus seems so real to you."

"Like a Friend not far away," Mrs. Fisher added.

"But how am I to know if He wants me to go to China or to stay in Bristol?"

Mrs. Fisher answered,

<table>
<tr><td>GUESS</td><td>1. "You can never know."
2. "He will show you."
3. "Have patience."</td></tr>
</table>

Mrs. Fisher whispered, "Trust God, have patience, and He will show you."

Gladys stayed with the Fishers until they both died

<table>
<tr><td>GUESS</td><td>1. five years later.
2. one year later.
3. two years later.</td></tr>
</table>

Gladys spent two years in Bristol. She came back to London a strong Christian. "Mum," she said, "I could never have had better Bible teachers or better missionary training anywhere."

"If you are so interested in missions," her mother said one day, "come with me to the Prim Street Missionary Society meeting to-night."

Gladys started to say, "I'm too tired," but something stopped her. "All right, Mum, I'll go," she said.

6

A Ticket

"I'm interested in China, too." An older woman grasped Gladys's hand after the missionary meeting. "A friend of a friend of mine has just gone back to China, where she worked for many years with her husband."

Gladys blinked, wondering what to say.

"She came home when her husband died. But when the Society failed to send anyone to take her place, she insisted on going back, even though she is seventy-three years old."

"Seventy-three," Gladys marveled. "And some folks say I'm too old at twenty-eight. What's her name?"

"Mrs. Lawson, and she prays every day for *someone* to come to take her place before she dies."

Gladys said,

GUESS	1. "A young man, perhaps?"
	2. "An experienced missionary?'
	3. "That's meant for me."

Gladys said, "That's why I've felt I should go. She needs me, she wants me, and God has called me."

"I'll write to her and ask," the older woman said.

Three months later a letter from China arrived at Gladys's home. Mrs. Lawson wrote,

GUESS	1. "Ask your friends to support you."
	2. "Apply to a missionary society."
	3. "I'll meet you in Tientsin."

Mrs. Lawson wrote, "I'll meet you in Tientsin if you can find your way out."

"Then all I need is a ticket," Gladys decided.

After church service Gladys told the pastor of the Prim Street church. He

GUESS	1. encouraged Gladys.
	2. discouraged Gladys.
	3. didn't care.

"No, no, you can't go!" the pastor commanded. "You must do things properly. Without a missionary society you will starve. You will have no home, no meeting place."

"I'll have God," Gladys defended herself. "He is enough!"

"Don't listen to that old Mrs. Lawson. She's crazy to encourage you. I think too much of your family to send you on a wild chase. Anyway, you have no ticket, so you'll stay here." The pastor was shaking hands with his congregation at the door and dismissed Gladys by reaching for the hand of his next member.

As they walked through the crowded London streets toward home, Gladys told her mother, "All I need to do is earn enough money for a ticket."

"How can you do that?"

"I'll go back to Mrs. Paddington if she'll have me," Gladys said.

Next day Gladys went to Drury Lane. Mrs. Paddington's greeting, "Come in, come in—I wondered what happened to you," encouraged her.

After a good visit, the young woman explained, "I'd like to make enough money for a ticket to China."

Mrs. Paddington's chin dropped, but she soon regained her poise. "Now that I have three children, I've been thinking of hiring a nanny. Since the children already like Alice, she could be the nanny. You could have your old job as a parlor maid." Her tone sounded so doubtful that Gladys said,

GUESS	1. "What's wrong?"
	2. "That's fine."
	3. "Why not?"

Gladys looked into Mrs. Paddington's eyes. "What's wrong? It sounds fine to me."

"Well, it's none of my business, but, Gladys, your plan sounds impractical. I don't think God would ask you to go to China without an organization to support you. How will you live?"

"If I knew the end from the beginning, I wouldn't need faith! Faith is enough for me." Determination filled Gladys's eyes.

"Very well, move your things into your old room. I have friends who hire extra help for parties and such. So there is plenty of work if you want it."

"Thank you. You won't be sorry!"

Gladys moved her few belongings the next day. As she left home, the younger children waved good-bye. "Gladys, you are

GUESS	1. crazy."
	2. smart."
	3. stupid."

"You're crazy, just crazy, Gladys. Why don't you get married like other girls?"

"I would if I found anyone like Father," Gladys retorted, "and someone who wants to go to China as a missionary."

Once she was settled in her tiny attic room at Mrs. Paddington's, Gladys arranged her things. She put the Bible with large print on her bed. Beside it she put her *Daily Light* devotional book and all her money, just a few cents.

Gladys knelt beside the plain bed. She read of Abraham's call, of Moses' burning bush. Aloud she prayed, "Oh, God, here's my Bible, here's my *Daily Light,* and here's all my money. If You want me, I'm going to China with these."

Alice poked her head in the door. "Are you clean crazy? Gabbing to yourself! The mistress wants you."

On her days off Gladys worked extra time at dinner parties. "Mrs. Paddington," she asked one day, "what is the cheapest fare to China, by ship or by train?"

"If you want the cheapest, it's by the railway, overland through Europe, Russia, and Siberia. You can buy a ticket in the Haymarket." Mrs. Paddington pressed her lips together and said no more, but her eyes disapproved.

On the next Tuesday, Gladys made her way to

GUESS	1. the Marble Arch.
	2. Royal Cross Station.
	3. the Haymarket.

By taking three different busses Gladys arrived at the Haymarket, one of the busiest places she had ever seen. People hurried everywhere. She tried to stop someone to ask for the train station. Then she saw it. "It's so big. I didn't realize it would take up a whole block. I was looking for a little counter."

She saw people lined up to buy tickets and joined the crowd. When her turn came, she asked, "How much will it cost for a single ticket to China?"

"China? China, did you say? Now come on, Miss, we haven't time for jokes. What do you want?"

"I want to go to China. Tientsin, China!"

"If You want me, I'm going to China with these."

"Well, I never! All right, I'll find out. It's in these books some-where, I suppose."

While the agent searched, the people behind Gladys com-plained, but Gladys held her place.

"The ticket costs £47.10 from London to Tientsin, but don't go. There is fighting in Manchuria. You'd never get through; it's too risky!"

Gladys put £3 on the counter. "That's all I have now, but every time I earn a pound, I'll bring it to you until I get all £47."

"Lady, you can't do that. We don't take no money till you have it all. Didn't you hear me? I said . . . don't go!" the agent shouted.

"God said to go." Gladys's eyes appeared to snap. "I do what He says, not you!"

Since Gladys didn't move, the people behind her began shout-ing, "Take the money, and let's move!"

Dazed, the agent accepted the £3, and Gladys walked away.

It took Gladys another

GUESS	1. two years.
	2. five years.
	3. ten years.

Gladys worked for another two years to earn the money for her ticket.

"Upon my soul! I never dreamed you'd make it that first day you came here." The ticket agent grinned. "I'll sell you the ticket, but my advice still is don't go!"

Father took Gladys and her belongings to the Liverpool Street Station on October 15, 1932, but he could not bear to see her off. In fact, he barely said good-bye as he hurried away.

So Gladys set off for China

GUESS	1. alone.
	2. with a few friends.
	3. with a crowd waving.

41

Almost fifty friends gathered to see Gladys off.

"Do you have everything?" they asked.

"Yes. Mother sewed secret pockets in my coat for my ticket and my passport. Also, my big-print Bible and glass are here, thanks to Reverend Fisher."

"What about money?" Violet asked.

"I have two traveler's checks, worth one pound each, and my fountain pen, all sewed in safely."

"Here's a new suitcase," her friends said. "We packed it with crackers, cookies, tins of corned beef, baked beans, fish, meat cubes, coffee, tea, and hard-boiled eggs. You won't have to spend any money for food."

Gladys looked at all her baggage. "How can I carry all this?"

"We'll help you get it on the train. As you eat the things in the suitcase, you'll have room for some of this other stuff," Violet volunteered.

Gladys looked at her other things—an old army blanket, a bedroll, teakettle, saucepan, and a small stove.

"Thank you," she said as she boarded the train. She wore

GUESS	1. a reefer coat. 2. an orange frock. 3. a homemade cap.

"God bless you!" her friends cried over and over again, looking atGladys in her orange dress and cap.

Just before the train started, Gladys looked up as a woman from the Prim Street church hurried down the aisle.

"Gladys, Gladys! You're going into cold country. Here, take my fur coat." The woman shoved the coat at Gladys and fled from the train as the whistle blew.

"As if I didn't already have too much to carry!" Gladys wept, not because of the coat, but because she

| GUESS |

1. was sorry to go.
2. hated to leave her family.
3. was afraid of the future.

"Oh, Father, Mum—everyone! How can I leave you?" she cried.

7

A Journey

"**C**lickity-clack, clickity-clack." The wheels of the steam en-gine rattled across England. Gladys feasted her eyes on the scenery as it flew by her window.

"Pardon me, Miss," an attractive English woman said. "I couldn't help seeing the send-off your friends gave you. Where are you going?"

"To China to be a missionary," Gladys said happily.

"By yourself?"

"Yes."

"My dear, have you any idea of the danger? You'll be fine on this train, and, indeed, for several days, but then you'll transfer to the Trans-Siberian line through Russia. Do you know how long that line is?"

"No." Gladys looked confused.

"It's

GUESS	1. one thousand miles." 2. six thousand miles." 3. three thousand miles."

"It's 6,300 miles from the Polish border to Vladivostok, the largest railway system in the world."

"Really. Well, I knew it must be a long way to cost so much, but I can ride along. I have plenty of food." Gladys refused to be discouraged.

"Once you reach the point where no one speaks English you'll have trouble. I've heard of people who went to Russia and never returned. They have slave labor camps, you know."

"Oh, well, I'm British. Nothing will happen to me."

"You don't know

GUESS

1. the Russians."
2. the danger."
3. the war."

"The Russians will take your money, and you, too, if they can."

"Well, they can't. God won't let them." Gladys appeared unmoved, her dark eyes peaceful.

"And the war between Japan and China is far from over," the woman persisted. "I hear the trains don't run in Manchuria, where you are headed."

"Oh, well, they gave me a ticket. They must have some way to get there."

"I wish I were so optimistic." The woman sighed.

When she left the train, she gave Gladys

GUESS

1. six cents.
2. one pound.
3. ten cents.

The woman's husband pressed a pound note into Gladys's hand.

For miles Gladys debated about a hiding place for the money. Suddenly she remembered her

GUESS	1. umbrella.
	2. shoes.
	3. hat.

"Mother cut layers of felt to put in my boots since they were too big. I'll put this note between the layers," Gladys decided as the train rolled on and on.

She could not know this note would some day save

GUESS	1. her shoes.
	2. her life.
	3. her time.

Her very life would some day depend on this one bill.

At night Gladys curled her hair, put on a nightcap, and slept. Being small, she could curl up on her seat. The train passed Berlin, Warsaw, Moscow, and skirted Lake Baikal.

On her seventh day, October 22, 1932, she crossed into Siberia. There she changed trains.

I must get outside for a minute, she said to herself. *I need to stretch my legs.*

Gladys leaped to the platform and walked to the front of the new train. She stared at the enormous black engine with a red star on a large white circle. But when the icy wind struck her, she turned back. "Oh, it is freezing. I must hurry inside."

As soon as the men finished sawing huge chunks of wood, loading them, and filling the boilers with water, the Siberian Express puffed down the tracks.

Gladys ate a tin of beans and made a cup of tea. She offered some to a nearby woman, who only shook her head.

During these lonely days, Gladys

GUESS	1. wrote letters.
	2. kept a journal.
	3. sang songs.

Gladys kept a journal of her adventures.

At Chita, Gladys noticed that only soldiers remained on the train. Two Russian soldiers approached her and talked rapidly in their language. They pointed to her baggage and to the train door. They pointed to her, then to the outside.

They think they can put me off! Well, they can't! Gladys thought. When each of the two soldiers picked her up by an arm and started toward the door, Gladys

GUESS	1. kicked them.
	2. bit them.
	3. shot them.

Gladys kicked and bit them so savagely that they finally put her down. The train rolled on. When night fell, the engine stopped. The soldiers left, and Gladys sat silently waiting.

After an hour, she walked through the entire train. She found

GUESS	1. sick people.
	2. wounded soldiers.
	3. no one.

Gladys found no one. Soon blackness covered everything, even the station. Fumbling through her things, she pulled out her fur coat. In the pocket she found a wool stocking cap and a scarf. Wrapping herself in these, she prayed, "Oh, God, I'm thousands of miles from home, here in a Siberian snowbank, but You're not thousands of miles away. Help me, please!"

She slept so soundly that she didn't hear

GUESS	1. wolves.
	2. gunfire.
	3. the howling wind.

Gladys didn't hear the gunfire of war nearby.

In the morning she repacked her things so that she could drag them behind her.

First she explored the empty station. "Oho, someone is here," she cried aloud.

She discovered four men in a nearby hut.

When she knocked on the door, they let her in to warm herself by their fire.

The engineer pointed down the track ahead of the train. He popped his hands together, saying, "Bang! Bang! Boom!" The fear in his eyes told Gladys of

GUESS	1. wolves. 2. war. 3. gunfire.

"The war? The war?" she asked.

Not understanding her words, the guard pointed at the track in the direction the train had come. He jabbered in unknown words.

Then the porter seized Gladys's baggage and mimicked her dragging her things. They laughed and pointed down the line back to Chita.

When Gladys understood, she nodded her head. Gladys thought, *I*

GUESS	1. *should have stayed in Chita.* 2. *should have listened to the soldiers.* 3. *should not be so stubborn.*

My stubbornness is causing me to walk back.

She accepted a cup of strong coffee and prepared to go.

Gladys tied her bedroll across her shoulders. She took her suitcase by the handle and dragged everything else tied in the blanket. One of the men patted the fur coat, which she wore over her wool coat. He smiled and said,

48

```
┌─────────────┐   1. "Good luck."
│   GUESS     │   2. "Good-bye."
└─────────────┘   3. "Farewell."
```

Gladys couldn't understand his words, but she said good-bye and walked along the railway toward Chita.

At dusk Gladys put her suitcase down beside the tracks. She wrapped herself in her blanket and ate some stale crackers and cold sausage.

Then she lay down on top of her suitcase, with the fur coat wrapped around her. "If I don't freeze tonight, I'll go on tomorrow," she said, exhausted.

That night she was visited by

```
┌─────────────┐   1. wolves.
│   GUESS     │   2. bears.
└─────────────┘   3. angels.
```

Gladys never knew what came that night and ate her crackers and sausages. "I'm thankful they were satisfied without eating me!" she said the next morning. "It's too cold to sleep, so I'll be on my way."

She felt comfortable talking to herself. It helped her ignore the

```
┌─────────────┐   1. barking.
│   GUESS     │   2. howling.
└─────────────┘   3. growling.
```

Gladys ignored howling noises nearby. "I've heard wolves are afraid of strong people. I hope they think I'm strong and stay away."

Drops of fear slid down her spine as all day she could hear something trailing her. "I wonder why I never see them. Anyway, they keep me from feeling too tired. I must not stop."

Just as Gladys began to feel frantic, she saw the evening lights of Chita. "I'm thankful I didn't give up."

With her last efforts, she pulled herself up to the train platform. She looked

GUESS	1. dirty.
	2. untidy.
	3. tired.

Cold, stiff, and so tired that she could hardly stagger down the platform, Gladys stopped when she saw a soldier. He directed her to walk ahead of him, but she could no longer carry her baggage.

"I will not go without it," she tried to explain.

Angrily he shouted at her until three more soldiers appeared, and one picked up her bags. One, who wore a red hat, looked like an official. The others grabbed her and marched her to a place of filth and stench. Cold perspiration gathered on her forehead. *This must be their jail,* she thought. They tried to get her to eat, but she was so ill she could not.

"Here, here is my passport. See? I'm a British citizen. See?" she pleaded.

They removed her coat and

GUESS	1. slashed open the secret pockets.
	2. stole her money.
	3. gave her a new coat.

She watched as they slashed open the secret pockets of her coat and took her money and magnifying glass. In a daze she saw them laugh at each other's big noses in the glass.

When they found her Bible, they flung it at her. A piece of cardboard fell to the floor. Gladys read the large print, "Be ye not afraid of them. I am your God."

Quickly Gladys reached down to pick up the Bible. Her legs buckled under her, and she fell forward, unconscious.

8
Russia

The next morning Gladys awoke when two soldiers roughly lifted her from the bed. *Oh, how it smells here—like an outside toilet!* she thought. Vaguely she remembered being tossed on the bed, her coats thrown over her.

The soldiers hurried her down a long corridor. Ahead of her she noticed another Russian soldier about to drink from a cup. After one look at Gladys, he forced the cup into her hands. Gladys

GUESS	1. drank tea.
	2. drank coffee.
	3. refused to drink.

Gladys drank the cold tea and felt somewhat revived as she entered a large barren hall. On a table she noticed all her belongings laid out, minus the two English pounds and the magnifying glass.

I wish I could understand what they are saying, she thought. *They seem to have a problem knowing what to do with me.* She saw one soldier leafing through her Bible. Suddenly he cried out and held up a picture.

I'd forgotten about my brother's picture in his army band uniform, Gladys thought as the soldiers examined the print. *Why should that excite them so?* Then she realized that they were looking at his uniform. *So much gold braid and the many brass buttons must impress them. They think my brother is someone important in the British army.* Gladys smiled.

That smile and the picture produced a change. Respectfully, the officer showed her a map with Chita clearly marked. With his finger he pointed to a detour to Pogranilchnai. The officer gave her

GUESS	1. a new visa.
	2. another ticket.
	3. a kick.

The leader presented Gladys with a new visa and ticket. He even helped her onto the right train. However, he kept many of her things, including the fur coat.

Two days later Gladys reached Pogranilchnai. Here she found the same problem. "I wish to go to Harbin," she said, but received only shrugs and shaking heads in response. Showing her tickets produced only sneers and snarls.

At night she sat in the cold station. By day pale sunlight lured her to the platform. Once she saw fifty people—men, women, and young girls—chained together by their hands and feet. Communist guards drove the hysterical people along. She guessed they were being taken to

GUESS	1. slave labor camps.
	2. Siberia.
	3. England.

Seeing their misery filled Gladys with a hatred for Communism. *I must get out of here before they get me, too,* she thought.

As trains slowed at the station, Gladys examined the faces of people looking out the windows. "Oh, there's a man who looks English." She yelled loudly, "Sir, how can I get to Harbin?"

52

The train moved away slowly, but the man shouted in English, "You can't—it's blocked. Go to Vladivostok!"

"Thank you." *Now I know what to do.* "Thank You, God!" she breathed.

She returned to the ticket agent and said, "Vladivostok, Vladivostok." This time she received

GUESS	1. a shrug.
	2. a blank stare.
	3. a ticket.

Gladys took her ticket and rushed to the train. It was overcrowded, so she had to wait for six hours until the next one arrived.

While riding along Gladys suddenly remembered a

GUESS	1. friend.
	2. poster.
	3. song.

"I saw a poster once in a London station." Gladys tried to picture it in her mind. *See Russia through Intourist.* "I don't know what Intourist is, but I'll ask. Surely someone there will speak English," she said.

At the Vladivostok train station, Gladys stopped everyone who would listen. She cried, "Intourist, Intourist."

Finally a man helped her carry her things to an office. Quickly he disappeared before Gladys could thank him.

The gentleman behind the counter could indeed speak some Engish. "You need a hotel!" he stated. Gladys looked at herself—filthy coat, dirty orange dress, smelly body. "You are right. I do need a hotel, but I have no money."

"Never mind. We have a fund for stranded tourists. Come with me."

Gladys

GUESS	1. refused. 2. followed. 3. asked questions.

Gladys asked no questions. Gratefully she followed him to a fourth-floor hotel room. As soon as he departed, after promising to return the next day, Gladys bathed and washed her clothes. Then she opened one of her tins of fish. At last she slept.

Next morning Gladys washed her hair and put on her damp underclothes. "This orange dress is a mess. My washing didn't get the stains out, and it needs ironing." Since it was all she had, however, she put it on again. "I feel like a new person," she added, as she surveyed herself in the small mirror.

Carefully she folded her train tickets and visa and put them into her dress pocket. "Too bad the secret pockets in my coat are all slashed."

Suddenly Gladys looked around at her things. "Where is my passport? My British passport! Where, oh, where is it?" Frantically Gladys searched. She finally concluded,

GUESS	1. "It's lost!" 2. "It's stolen!" 3. "It's here!"

"The Intourist man must have taken it when he brought me here," Gladys said aloud. She heard

GUESS	1. a knock. 2. a shout. 3. a whistle.

A knock at the door sent Gladys hurrying to open it. Relieved, she saw the gentle little man from Intourist. "Sir, did you take my passport last evening?"

54

"Oh, that. Yes, I took it for safekeeping. Come with me, and we'll have breakfast together."

His smile put Gladys at ease, and breakfast sounded wonderful. She followed him to the hotel dining room and gladly ate slabs of pork, eggs, and large rolls with hard crusts.

"We are going back to the Intourist office. The manager wishes to speak with you," the kind man informed Gladys.

As they walked along the street edged with shops, she guessed, "This is a seaport. I smell the ocean air and see the gulls."

"Yes, a port on the Sea of Japan," her guide admitted.

Once Gladys faced the manager, she began, "Sir, how am I to get to Tientsin?"

"You cannot go there. The trains cannot get through because of the war. You say you have no money. Stay here and help us." The manager sounded kind but very firm.

"Why?"

"We need new people," he answered.

"No! I will not stay here. You don't need *me!*"

"We do need people who can handle machines, teachers who can train factory workers," he went on.

"But I know nothing of machines!" Gladys objected. "Where did you get such an idea?"

"Your passport says you are a machinist."

"No! No! You do not understand. It says I'm a missionary, not a machinist!"

"You stay in Russia. We look after you. You find fine Russian husband!" The manager stood up as though the interview were over.

"But I'm expected in China!" A cold fear gripped Gladys. She tried to say more, but the guide hurried her from the room.

"They can't do this to me! They can't!" Gladys raved, but the guide took her to

GUESS	1. a factory.
	2. the train station.
	3. the hotel.

55

Gladys found herself back in the hotel room. The little man warned her as he left. "Remember, you have no money, no friends. You can do nothing!"

9

Unknown Friends

Gladys worried and prayed, then prayed and worried. Finally she grew hungry and opened her last can of corned beef.

"My food will soon be gone, and then what will I do? I hope that lady from Holland is praying every night, like she said she would. She tried to warn me. She even said we would meet in heaven, if not on this earth. Hm." Gladys washed down the last of the corned beef with water. "We may meet sooner than we thought." Gladys shook herself.

"But I must do something! I'll

GUESS	

1. run away."
2. send a telegram."
3. go for a walk."

"At least the sun is shining, and I can go for a walk," Gladys decided. "God will show me a way, somehow."

As she stepped outside the hotel and closed the door, a young woman walked beside her. "Who are you?" Gladys asked.

"Never mind," the young woman said in English. "You want to leave here?"

Gladys nodded.

"If you don't get out now, you will never get away." The girl paused. "I know!" She looked into Gladys's eyes with the sadness of an old, old woman.

"But how can I get away?"

"Listen carefully. Get your things together. When an old crippled man knocks at your door early in the morning, ask no questions. Follow him silently."

At the next corner, the girl disappeared before Gladys could find out more information. Gladys kept on walking. *How do I know I can trust her?* she wondered.

Gladys glanced casually at the shop windows on the tall buildings. When she came to the end of the street, she could see the ocean.

"What a beautiful bay—the Sea of Japan! Imagine me here!" She noticed the sun shining on the waves, so crystal clear. Patches of snow clung to the edges of the streets, but the water was not frozen. Ships and boats filled the port.

"That's what I need." Gladys sighed. "A ship to Japan, then China. Oh, Jesus, help me!" She remembered the Bible verse "Be not afraid. Remember I am the Lord."

More hopeful, she returned to the hotel. After undressing she heard a knock on the door.

Gladys threw her blanket around her and opened the door a crack. The man from Intourist, obviously drunk, held out

| GUESS | 1. a fur coat.
| | 2. a passport.
| | 3. a ticket.

"My passport!" Gladys shouted and grabbed it from his hand. Quickly she threw it backward into the room and tried to shut the door. She smelled liquor and felt the man try to force the door open.

"You are not coming in here!" she said.

"Why not?"

58

"This is my bedroom!"

"But I'm the master. Did I not pay for the room? You shall do what I say."

"You cannot come in here." Gladys stretched herself to her full five feet. "God is here. He puts a barrier between you and me. Go!" Gladys glared angrily at the man. "Go!" she repeated.

The man

GUESS	1. stayed.
	2. left.
	3. argued.

Slowly the little man withdrew his foot from the door, and Gladys slammed and locked it.

Trembling, she threw all her belongings together. Almost everything would now fit into the suitcase, so that her bundle was small. She dressed and again lay on the bed while she looked at her passport.

"They really did change 'missionary' to 'machinist,' " she marveled. "The girl was right. I must leave here at once."

That night Gladys

GUESS	1. slept.
	2. prayed.
	3. sang.

Gladys slept little, for she knew only God could save her. "Oh, Lord Jesus, I've done all I can. Now it's up to You."

Early in the morning Gladys heard a light tap on the door. Instantly she jumped to her feet and peeped out to see a crippled old man. Without a word, he took her suitcase. Gladys put on her cloth coat and picked up her bundle.

Together they slipped by the sleeping night clerk into the street. Up and down they trudged on the rough cobblestones. *We've walked a hundred miles,* Gladys thought. Finally she saw the docks.

When the sky lightened, Gladys could see a ship. The old man left, and the girl from the hotel appeared. "Have you anything of value?" she questioned.

"No, nothing. Everything was taken."

"Well, you *must* get on that boat. Go to that shack, beg, plead with the captain. Sign anything, do anything, but *get on* the boat!"

"Why are you helping me?" Gladys asked.

"Because you need help! Now go!"

"Can I give you something?"

"Clothes." The girl shivered.

"Here, take these gloves and stockings. They are old but warm."

The girl snatched the clothing and fled.

Gladys pushed open the door of the small shack. A Japanese captain was sitting there alone. "I must get on your ship!" she pleaded.

"Stop! Speak slowly!" the captain ordered. "Now, what can I do for you?"

"Take me to Japan on your boat!"

"Do you have money—valuables?"

"No, nothing. But I'm British; see my passport."

The captain examined her passport carefully. "I see you are in trouble! Will you sign papers saying you are my prisoner?"

"Yes, anything," Gladys answered, signing the papers the captain produced.

"We leave at once!" the captain said. "Hurry after me. Soldiers come behind you."

The captain strode ahead. Gladys hurried up the gangplank. Two soldiers caught her as she ran. Almost to the deck, Gladys threw her suitcase and bundle on board. Suddenly, she remembered

GUESS	1. her passport.
	2. her ticket.
	3. the money in her shoe.

"The money in my shoe!" she cried. "I'd forgotten it." Swiftly she pulled out the pound note and flung it at the soldiers. The wind lifted it over their heads. "Look! I buy myself off!"

One soldier turned back to catch the bill, but the other clasped Gladys's arm. With a mighty jerk that tore the arm off her cloth coat, Gladys escaped up the gangplank just as the ship began to move.

The captain of the ship

GUESS

1. imprisoned Gladys.
2. turned her over to missionaries.
3. sent her home.

When the ship reached Japan, the captain turned Gladys over to the British missionaries there. They

GUESS

1. took up a collection.
2. sent Gladys to China.
3. sent her back to Russia.

The missionaries took up a collection and sent Gladys by ship across the Yellow Sea to Tientsin, China. They also sent a message to Mrs. Lawson.

When the ship docked, Gladys heard a voice. "Mrs. Lawson, she busy in mountains. She send me to meet you." A tiny young Chinese man welcomed Gladys amidst the crowds on the dock.

Gladys smiled. "My name's Gladys Aylward. What's your name?"

"Mr. Lu. I'm native pastor who preaches in Lawson church. This way, please."

Together they boarded a bus to another town, where Gladys was

GUESS

1. robbed.
2. welcomed by missionaries.
3. given new clothes.

61

Two soldiers caught her as she ran.

"You must be frozen in those clothes!" The missionary ladies fussed over Gladys. "Come inside; we are waiting dinner for you."

After Gladys enjoyed a good night's rest in a clean bed, the ladies gave her some Chinese clothes. "These things would have been worn out long ago, but they were too small for most missionaries. Like Cinderella's slipper, they fit you, and you shall have them."

"Oh, thank you!" Gladys said. "No one could need them more."

When Mr. Lu brought a mule to the door, Gladys said, "You say I have to ride on this mule to get to Yangcheng?" Gladys climbed on the mule, but she did not tell them, "I'm from the city. I know nothing of animals."

"It's only for two days." The friendly missionaries smiled, then they added slowly, "Honey, we wish you every blessing. Mrs. Lawson's mind comes and goes. We will pray you can get along with her. No one else can."

Now Gladys wondered if she were more afraid of the mule or of Mrs. Lawson.

10
Mules

After crossing three mountain ranges and fording numerous rivers, Gladys's bones ached, and she realized mules are

GUESS
1. stubborn.
2. surefooted.
3. mean.

"Mules are so stubborn," she said to Mr. Lu.

"Like some people!"

"Like me!" Gladys laughed. "But I'm trying to change. Tell me, aren't we almost there?"

"Yes. See gateway? That's entrance to Yangcheng. We stop now."

Gladys slid off her mule, walking painfully. "I'm so stiff and sore. I hope I never ride a mule again!"

"Oh, you will—many times," Mr. Lu said.

"What a dirty place!" Gladys gasped, noting rooms with no doors or windows. "Just holes in the walls. And litter everywhere!"

"You see, Mrs. Lawson just move to this abandoned inn. See the large courtyard with the long lodge for the muleteers and stables for many mules. She think we clean it up and open soon."

"Oh," Gladys said, following Mr. Lu to Mrs. Lawson's door. She felt

GUESS

1. untidy.
2. fearful.
3. shy.

Gladys felt shy and fearful as she stepped into the doorway.

"And who are you?" asked a tall, thin lady with curly white hair and glasses.

"I'm Gladys Aylward. Remember? You wrote for me to come!"

"Oh, yes, I'd almost forgotten. Well, are you coming in or not?"

Gladys stepped inside, noting the rubbish everywhere.

"I suppose you are hungry," Mrs. Lawson said, dipping strange food into a bowl. Since Gladys saw no table or chairs, she took the bowl and sat on the floor. She noticed Mrs. Lawson's blue eyes measuring her from behind her glasses.

"There isn't much of you, I see. No matter—you won't need much to eat, then!" the silver-haired woman observed.

Gladys looked at her food, smelled it, and slowly put it into her mouth. *Oh, it tastes horrible,* she thought, but tried not to show her dislike.

Mrs. Lawson explained, "This place is old, in a poor part of town, but it's empty, and the rent's cheap—about thirty cents a year. No Chinese will live here because they say it is haunted. I haven't seen any ghosts myself. I'm trying to clean up, but I'm so weak."

Since Gladys was hungry, she was able to eat about half the food before she pushed it aside. "May I go to bed?" Gladys asked. "I'm so tired."

"Oh, yes, you do as you wish."

"But where do I sleep?"

"Oh, anywhere! Anywhere you like."

Gladys stepped into the courtyard. Many rooms opened onto the square. Gladys chose one, swept the litter to one side, and put down her bedroll. She looked around, no glass in the windows, no curtains, no door.

She went back into Mrs. Lawson's room. "Where do I undress? I want to go to bed."

"Oh, I wouldn't bother to undress," Mrs. Lawson explained. "And it's safer to put all your things on your bed. That way nothing will be stolen."

Gladys returned to her room. *If no one is here, who is to steal?* she wondered, and went to bed without a bath. She thought,

GUESS	1. *What a welcome!*
	2. *I wish I were home.*
	3. *I'm too tired to care.*

Gladys, too sore and tired to care, prayed. Sleep overcame her worries.

When she opened her eyes to a bright morning, she saw every window and door crowded with

GUESS	1. curtains.
	2. faces.
	3. fog.

Dozens of faces stared at her. *I must be a freak to them,* she thought. *At least I have my clothes on. I'm thankful for that.*

She stepped outside, and Mrs. Lawson motioned for Gladys to walk with her to the gateway of the courtyard. Together they sat down on rocks outside the gate.

"Oh, Yangcheng is beautiful." Gladys beamed, gazing at the high mountains towering on either side of the valley. She noted the wall all around the city, the narrow winding streets, and numerous temples. "It must be a hundred years old."

"More than that—and little changed." Mrs. Lawson smiled a little. "You see why I had to come back. I love it so."

Gladys mused, "And to think I left London only five-and-a-half weeks ago. It seems an eternity. This place looks like a fairyland."

"No fairyland this." Mrs. Lawson sniffed. "Come, we have work to do!"

On the way back to her room, Mrs. Lawson outlined her plans.

"We are on the famous mule track from Hopeh to Honan. Long mule trains pass through every day. At night they stop in inns along the way. I intend to open this inn again. The muleteers only need a place on that long brick bed built down the side of the lodge. They will need a meal of millet and flour strips for themselves and fodder for the beasts."

"But who will cook?"

"We'll hire a Chinese cook for a few cents. I know one who comes to the church my husband started. Then, when the men are fed, we can talk to them about Christ."

"But how do we get them to come in here, especially if they think it is haunted?"

"You don't understand. I'll tell you in a minute." Mrs. Lawson motioned with her hand for Gladys to step into her room ahead of her.

When Mrs. Lawson entered, Gladys

GUESS	1. stood.
	2. ran away.
	3. sat on the floor.

They each took a bowl of food and sat on the earthen floor.

"Where was I?" Mrs. Lawson looked lost. "I was saying something important."

"You were telling me how to get the mule train to stop at the inn."

"Oh, yes. The Chinese landlord stands outside the gateway, where we sat a few minutes ago. He smiles—don't forget that. Then he grabs the first mule in the train by his long neck hairs. He drags him into the courtyard, and the rest of the mules follow. Since the muleteers are too tired to argue, they stay all night and pay well."

"But," Gladys objected, "if the cook is busy—and you are too old—who will pull the mules inside?"

"That's your job!"

"My job?" Gladys stared, horrified. "But I came to be a missionary!"

"Well, if you can't help, you may as well go home. Don't you see? Once the muleteers are fed, we can give them the gospel. They go everywhere in China. If they believe, they will tell everyone."

Gladys looked into the steely blue eyes. "Do mules bite?" she asked.

"Not if you grab the right part."

While Mrs. Lawson was gone to hire the cook, Gladys cleaned. Since curious villagers watched, Gladys motioned for them to help.

"Well, I wouldn't call it clean," Mrs. Lawson said on her return. "But it certainly looks better."

To Gladys's surprise the cook, Mr. Yang, spoke some English. "What do you say to get the muleteers to come in?" she asked.

"You yell loudly, '*Meiyu ch'ouse, meiyu ke'tsao! Hao, hao, hao! Lai, lai, lai!*' "

When Gladys repeated his words perfectly, the cook said, "You know Chinese."

"Oh, no, but I mimic. What do the words mean?" Gladys asked.

"Mimic—what's that?"

"Copy. Say as you say." Gladys tried to explain. "But what did I say?"

"You say, 'We have no bedbugs. We have no fleas. Good, good, good. Come, come, come.' Say it again," Mr. Yang directed.

After Gladys repeated the words perfectly, the cook smiled. "You learn Chinese quick, quick, before Mrs. Lawson die."

11
Feet

The "Inn of Eighth Happiness," as Mrs. Lawson called their compound, soon was known throughout North China. The muleteers said, "The foreign ladies are clean, the food is good, and at night they tell long stories free."

Gladys listened to Mrs. Lawson tell Bible stories over and over. She saw men give their hearts and lives to Jesus. In six months' time, she understood the language. By the year's end, she could

| GUESS | 1. preach.
2. repeat stories.
3. sing. |

Gladys sang familiar songs in Chinese, but the remarkable thing to Mr. Yang was that she could repeat the Bible stories and lessons, word for word, exactly as Mrs. Lawson told them.

She wrote home, "The language is difficult, but it's like this: if you have to speak Chinese, you speak Chinese."

One day while Mrs. Lawson lay sick, Gladys noticed her glasses in the kitchen. *I'd like to try them on,* she thought, picking them up.

One look through the lens, however, and she was horrified. "They make it worse," she said, but before taking them off, she put a hand over one eye.

Suddenly everything was clear! She ran to her room and pulled out her Bible. Gladys

GUESS	1. could not see.
	2. could see.
	3. cried.

"Yes, I can see the words. I can read with one eye and the glasses." Gladys pranced around her room.

One year later Mrs. Lawson called Gladys to her bed. "God called you to my side in answer to my prayers. He wants you to carry on His work here. He will provide. He will bless and protect you."

Within a week, Mrs. Lawson died at the age of

GUESS	1. seventy-three.
	2. seventy-four.
	3. eighty-four.

Mrs. Lawson died when she was seventy-four. When Mr. Lu preached her funeral service, Gladys understood every word. She wept.

"Now what will we do?" Mr. Lu, Mr. Yang, and Gladys gathered in the lodge after the funeral.

"You two must be paid from the fees we collect from muleteers," Gladys said firmly.

"Then there's nothing for you, and you shouldn't tend mules, scraping mud, feeding them, and cleaning stalls." Mr. Lu looked at Gladys. "I always hated it when Mrs. Lawson made you do it."

"It has to be done." Gladys was matter-of-fact. "The truth is that without the money Mrs. Lawson's friends sent from England, we cannot all live here."

Mr. Yang suggested, "Then you must go and

70

GUESS	1. get a job."
	2. bow to the mandarin."
	3. steal money."

"Why? Why should I bow to the mandarin?" Gladys exploded. "How many times do you bow? What do you wear? I wouldn't know what to say to so important a man in the city."

Three days later a man came through the inn gateway. With a smile on his face, he walked ahead of three soldiers. His scarlet robes and cap were of satin, his sleeves wide and sweeping. He was the

GUESS	1. king.
	2. mandarin.
	3. governor.

As usual, Gladys spoke before she thought. "You look like you just stepped from a Chinese antique scroll. Who are you?"

"I am the mandarin. I govern this part of China." He spoke precise Chinese.

"Oh." Suddenly Gladys remembered Mr. Yang's words. She bowed. "Welcome to the Inn of Eighth Happiness."

"Miss Aylward, I have come for help."

"My help?"

"Yes, about your big feet."

"But I only wear size three. I do not understand."

"I have a letter from our new government. It is decreed that the ancient custom of binding women's feet must cease."

"That's good! I agree." Gladys's head bobbed up and down.

"But the government is holding me responsible for stamping out the custom." The mandarin looked distressed.

"Oh."

"Oh, you say, but how can I enforce this? A man can't inspect women's feet! That's a woman's job!"

"But how does this affect me?" Gladys asked.

"In all this district there is no woman with unbound feet but you. You alone can be the inspector."

Gladys looked as dumbfounded as she felt.

"You must travel all over this part of Shansi. The government will give you a mule to ride, two soldiers to protect you from harm, and a small salary." The mandarin waited as Gladys thought it over.

Is this God's way of providing for me? she wondered. "You know I came to China to tell people about God," she said aloud. "If I inspect the women's feet, I'll use the time to tell about Jesus."

"Very well, I understand. Besides, I've heard that if a woman becomes a Christian, she will unbind her feet. So, no trouble."

"Then I accept." Gladys smiled.

"You will have a new name—*Ai-weh-deh*."

"A virtuous woman!" Gladys repeated the name in English. "The Bible speaks of a virtuous woman. I'm flattered. Thank you for the new name." Gladys bowed.

The mandarin

GUESS	1. laughed.
	2. cried.
	3. bowed.

After much bowing, the mandarin and soldiers left.

Mr. Lu ran into the courtyard. "I heard excitement. Is it true you are foot inspector?"

"Yes, dear Mr. Lu. It is God's provision. He sent me here. He has provided. You can preach to the muleteers, and now we can hire someone to care for the mules."

"How wonderful! You be safe with two guards. After inspections, you gather people for Bible stories."

"Oh, I will," Gladys said. "I'll tell them of

GUESS	1. Moses."
	2. Daniel."
	3. animals."

72

Gladys planned stories of Bible characters such as Moses and Daniel.

"But you will be called a foreign devil."

"Not for long. I look Chinese with my black hair pulled into a bun like theirs, my dark eyes, and my small body. Now that I speak Chinese, I think Chinese, too. I feel more Chinese now than British!"

"And you will come with the authority of the mandarin!"

For two years Gladys worked happily, until one day a messenger screamed as he ran into the town square,

GUESS	1. "Come to prison!"
	2. "Stop your work!"
	3. "You are fired!"

The messenger demanded that Ai-weh-deh and the soldiers go to the mandarin at the entrance of a prison.

"Why do you stop my work?" Gladys demanded as she approached the mandarin. She could hear cries of pain from the prison.

"The prisoners are rioting!"

"I hear them. Why?" Gladys asked.

"A convict went mad. See?" The mandarin pointed beyond the barred fence. "See that big man with the sharp ax attacking everyone? He has killed one or two already."

"Why don't you stop him?"

"I'm afraid. They'd kill me. That's why I need *you*. No one but you would dare to go in."

"Me?" Gladys gasped. "I'd *never* go in."

"But you say you have the God of Daniel, who went into the lion's den!"

"Yes, that's true, but I'm not Daniel!" Gladys's bottom lip shook as she spoke.

"But you have the same God to help you. You said so yourself."

Gladys looked a long time at the mandarin. "Well—" she said.

"Well, what? Is He the same God or not?"

73

Gladys said,

GUESS

1. "I won't go."
2. "I'll go."
3. "I'd be a fool to go!"

12
Prison

When the guards opened the prison door, Gladys stepped into the courtyard. A hush fell over the prisoners. A woman in a men's prison! Never!

Shouts and screams died. Gladys saw the madman coming toward her, eyes blazing and huge ax held ready to strike.

Gladys

GUESS

1. screamed.
2. fainted.
3. stood still.

Gladys stood stiff and stared into the madman's eyes. He came within a few feet of her and stopped, glaring.

In a mother's tone, Gladys said, "Give me that ax."

Madness died in the convict's eyes. He stepped forward, wiping the blood from the handle. He laid the ax in her hands.

"You must be tired," Gladys said. "Go lie on your bed." Slowly the madman walked away.

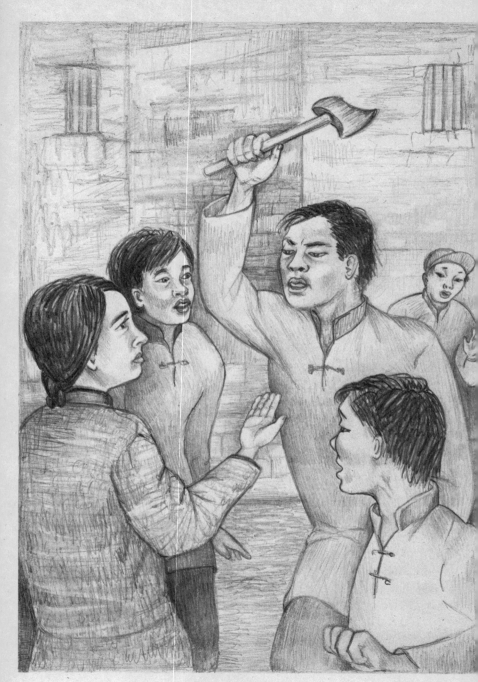

"Give me that ax."

After she handed the ax through the bars to the mandarin, Gladys's knees felt weak. She slumped to the ground and crossed her legs. "Sit down and tell me why this happened!"

She talked to the convicts for an hour. After hearing their stories, she said,

GUESS
1. "You should be ashamed."
2. "You are all crazy."
3. "I, too, would go mad."

"I, too, would go mad in such a place," Gladys said. "I'll talk to the mandarin. We'll see what can be done for you."

"Come back! Come back!" the prisoners called as she left the prison.

"I will—I promise!"

To the mandarin she said, "You're turning men into animals in such a prison, with nothing to do."

"What can they do? They're criminals! All prisons in China are like that. Why help these thieves?"

"If they could earn a living honestly, maybe they wouldn't be thieves."

"We don't know what to do." The mandarin looked at Gladys. "Do anything you like—go anywhere, talk, preach. It can't hurt!"

Gladys talked everything over with Mr. Lu and Mr. Yang.

"God works in wonderful ways." Mr. Lu beamed. "First, He made *church*. Then He gave work with *muleteers*."

Mr. Yang broke in, "Then He gave us Gladys to reach the *women* in the villages."

"And now," Gladys added, "He gives us work with

GUESS
1. children."
2. prisoners."
3. coolies."

Gladys said, "Now He has made a way for us to reach *prisoners*."

At their next meeting, Gladys said to the mandarin, "Put in weaving looms so the prisoners can make cloth and a miller's wheel so they can grind corn. Let them raise rabbits so they can pay off their debts and go free."

"Is that *all?*" The mandarin mocked her.

"No. Let them out of prison on Sunday so they can attend church."

"You mean so they can escape?" The mandarin laughed.

"They won't escape," Gladys assured him. "I'll ask them to behave."

The mandarin laughed again. "If *everyone* comes back to prison after church, I'll put in looms, a miller's wheel, and all you said."

"It's a fine bargain," Gladys cried.

"Not much of a gamble!" The mandarin grinned. "Some will escape—I know them."

After church services every Sunday, the prisoners

GUESS	1. escaped.
	2. returned.
	3. stayed in church.

Every prisoner returned to jail, and the mandarin kept his promise. Gladys rejoiced. "Thank You, God! You fulfill my heart's desires."

On her way home from church one Sunday, Gladys saw a shabby woman with her little girl. The child was thin and covered with sores. "Your child will die if you do not care for her," Gladys scolded the mother.

"You can have her if you like."

Gladys looked at the woman. "I don't believe in buying and selling children, but I'll *give* you ninepence. I don't want her to die."

"She's yours," the woman said, grasping the money in her bony fingers.

"Come little Ninepence," Gladys said, gently leading the child home to Happiness Inn. "You are mine now. I'll love you, care for you, and be a true mother to you."

This night Gladys was not lonely. She washed the girl and fed her in the kitchen.

"But what will you do when you have to make another inspection trip?" Mr. Yang objected as he dried his gleaming copper pans.

"Remember that new Christian, Mrs. Cheng, who lost her husband and children in a mud slide?"

"Yes."

"Please bring her here."

It was soon arranged, and Mrs. Cheng became a

GUESS	1. nursemaid.
	2. housekeeper.
	3. servant.

Gladys laughed. "I'm glad you will live with us. Your salary is small and your duties large, but you will be a mother to us."

Mrs. Cheng sniffed. "Only one child. I could care for twenty, so much love I have for little ones."

A few months later Ninepence found a boy running in the streets of Yangcheng. He had no mother, no father. She brought the boy home, and he

GUESS	1. died.
	2. hated Ninepence.
	3. brought two more.

He brought two more children to Gladys. And so it went until Mrs. Cheng did indeed have twenty children.

Mr. Yang put the older children to work helping in the inn. No mules ever got better treatment than the boys gave them. The girls served the muleteers food and sang at the story hour.

When Gladys came home from her foot-inspecting journeys, the children's eyes lit up with love for her.

"I am contented now," Gladys said. "I am really Chinese. I want to be a citizen."

79

When she asked for citizenship, the authorities

GUESS

1. refused.
2. accepted.
3. called her a foreign devil.

By now everyone knew Ai-weh-deh, the woman who stopped prison riots, the storyteller from Happiness Inn. She became a legal citizen under her new name.

"How happy I am," she told Mrs. Cheng. "I've worked for the mandarin for ten years. God has given me more converts than I could ever count if I tried. My children are healthy, and many have become Christians. You, too, Mrs. Cheng, are such a blessing. Everything is wonderful at Happiness Inn."

The next Sunday morning, while Gladys and the children were in town attending church, the silver airplanes came. Everyone in the village ran into the streets to see. "How lovely they look flying," the Chinese said.

But when bombs dropped, hundreds of citizens died. The mission house where Mr. Lu lived was hit. Gladys took her crying children home to Happiness Inn and hurried back to the village.

"What happened?" she cried, seeing the wounded dazed and still.

"The Japanese! War has finally come to Yangcheng!"

Gladys organized the Chinese to

GUESS

1. bury the dead.
2. attend the wounded.
3. look after the children.

Gladys organized all these activities while she herself comforted those who lost loved ones. She sent children who were left without family to Happiness Inn.

"But how can we feed them?" Mr. Yang asked. "You know you can't inspect feet with a war going on. You lose your salary. We have not enough food!"

Gladys touched Mr. Yang's hand. "You think God will fail us now?"

13
War Again

By 1938 the rulers of Yangcheng had changed four times. Every time the Chinese regained power, the Japanese bombed them and gained control again. During the fighting Gladys

GUESS
1. hid the children.
2. sent the children to the mountains.
3. gave them guns to fight.

Gladys took the children to the mountains, where they lived in caves or holes in the ground. They ate if they could find food. Gladys went everywhere begging for food and holding gospel meetings in Japanese or Chinese controlled districts. Both the Japanese and Chinese governments accepted her.

Since she knew where the Japanese troops were, she became valuable as a

GUESS
1. scout.
2. spy.
3. friend.

A Chinese general and his wife made friends with Gladys. "Tell us where the Japanese troops are," they entreated, "so we can send soldiers to capture them."

Gladys said,

GUESS

1. "I cannot take sides."
2. "Yes, I'll tell you."
3. "I want China to win."

Gladys gave information about Japanese troops because she wanted the Chinese to win the war.

She wrote one last letter to her mother before the postal system was destroyed. With tears running down her cheeks, she explained, "Life is pitiful, death so familiar, suffering and pain so common. Yet I would not be anywhere else. Do not wish me out of this, or in any way seek to get me out. These are my people, and I will live or die with them for Jesus' glory."

Three years later Gladys still hid in caves with the children. One day she had a visitor:

GUESS

1. the general.
2. the general's wife.
3. the mandarin.

Dressed in brown clothes, his braid cut off, the mandarin looked like an average Chinese.

"Why did you cut your queue?" Gladys asked. "I liked the long braid falling down your back."

"The Japanese hang you by your queue if they catch you. I'm glad to see you are still alive, Ai-weh-deh!" He took her hand. "I've come to say good-bye. I've watched you for a long time. You love our people and work hard for them. Only one filled with the spirit of the true God could do it."

"It is God's will," Gladys answered.

"Before I leave, I would like to be received into your church and worship your God. Will you grant it?"

83

"God will grant it. We'll all go back to Yangcheng. I hear the Chinese control it once more. Come, children."

They went to the church, where the mandarin provided one last feast. With the children gathered round, he spoke. "I have seen the spirit of God work through Ai-weh-deh and Mr. Lu. I want to be a Christian."

Mr. Lu sat down with his Chinese Bible and showed the mandarin

GUESS	1. the way to heaven.
	2. how to be good.
	3. Bible verses.

Together they read the Bible, and the mandarin prayed for forgiveness of his sins.

Gladys took the children to Happiness Inn. There they found

GUESS	1. ruins.
	2. a first-aid station.
	3. wounded soldiers.

Forty or more wounded soldiers lay in the courtyard. The place was in ruins. Walls were broken. Trash was everywhere.

"Mrs. Cheng, take the children to Christian homes in the village," Gladys directed.

Gladys washed, bandaged, and fed the soldiers until they were taken to their camps.

Mr. Yang returned to reopen the Inn as more muleteers than usual passed through. "So glad to see you alive!" he greeted Gladys. "I have news. The muleteers tell me Madame Chiang Kai-shek has opened orphanages in temples, colleges, anywhere—to care for homeless children. She has many gifts of money from America."

"I'll write to her today," Gladys promised, as she wrung out washrags. They looked at each other helplessly. "But we will do what we can, and God will do the rest."

Gladys wrote a letter to Madame Chiang Kai-shek and felt fortunate to get a reply. She read it aloud to

| GUESS |
1. Mr. Yang.
2. Violet.
3. the mandarin.

Gladys put on Mrs. Lawson's glasses, placed a hand over one eye, and read to Mr. Yang and Mr. Lee, "If you can bring the children into Free China to Shensi, we will look after them."

"Someone must take them at once," Gladys said.

"Do you realize we have more than one hundred children now?" Mr. Yang exclaimed. "Every time parents are killed by the enemy, the neighbors say, 'Take the children to Ai-weh-deh.' "

"Mr. Lu—" Gladys hesitated. "Would you lead the children to Shensi? I can work with the muleteers while you are gone." She added, "I know it will be a hard journey, maybe take two weeks. In a month's time you could be back."

"Very well, but we should start at once." Mr. Lu looked serious. "One never knows how this war goes. I hear the Communists are fighting in the north."

"The Communists? They are in Russia," Gladys protested.

"Not all of them. Many Chinese in the north are now Communists."

"You mean the Chinese are fighting Chinese?"

"I'm afraid so." Mr. Lu shook his head.

"What will you do for food on your journey?" Mr. Yang asked. "We must be practical."

"The mandarin left some food with me," Mr. Lu answered. "About enough for two days."

"After that you will have to beg." Gladys sighed.

"I know." Mr. Lu made a face. "I hate to beg."

The children thought the trip would be

GUESS

1. fun.
2. exciting.
3. awful.

The children thought the trip would be fun. They waved gaily to Gladys as they began the journey.

Two months later Mr. Lu

GUESS

1. returned.
2. had not returned.
3. was killed.

More children came. Gladys sent them on to a safe place.

"I wonder what is keeping Mr. Lu." Gladys worried one evening. "I wish he were here. The war is getting closer all the time. Come, Ninepence, let us kneel and pray. Only God can save us."

They had no sooner said amen when they heard

GUESS

1. a shout.
2. a knock.
3. a cry.

"Who is there?"

"I am a Christian soldier," a young man said as he strode into the room. "Ai-weh-deh, you must retreat!"

"No, my place is here!"

"The general sends word, pleads, 'Come!' The Japanese will take Yangcheng tonight. They want you!"

"Why me?"

The soldier showed her a poster. "These posters are everywhere."

Wanted. Ai-weh-deh. Spy.
Dead or Alive.
Reward.
£100 from Japanese High Command.

"Think it over. Many would betray you for a hundred pounds."

Back in her room, Gladys took out her Bible and Mrs. Lawson's glasses. Putting a hand over one eye, she read by the light of a candle,

GUESS	1. "He careth for you."
	2. "Flee ye, flee ye into the mountains."
	3. "Trust in the Lord."

She let the Bible fall open, and she read, "Flee ye, flee ye into the mountains."

"All right, Lord, I'll go. I'm not as stubborn as I once was. I'll go in the morning."

At daybreak Gladys looked through a peephole. "Oh, they are here already. I'll have to escape through the back gate."

As she slipped out the back, the Japanese came in the front. Someone spied Gladys as she crossed a stream and headed for an open field. The Japanese sent

GUESS	1. messengers.
	2. bullets.
	3. arrows.

Bullets flew around her head. She took off her padded jacket, threw it aside, and crawled under a bush. Bullets riddled the jacket. Gladys remained quiet for a long time, then she ran, fell, got up, and scrambled forward. She crawled, climbed, and finally lay exhausted beside the road to the mountains.

"Good-bye, Happiness Inn," she sobbed.

14
Life or Death

After two days of running and hiding, Gladys stumbled into the caves where the children hid. "Where is Mrs. Cheng?" she asked after hugging the children.

"Mrs. Cheng is

GUESS

1. gone."
2. sick."
3. hiding."

"She is sick," Ninepence said. "Come."

Oh, she looks horrible, Gladys thought as she tried to cover the shaking woman with a blanket.

"My brother will come for me soon," Mrs. Cheng whispered. "I've done all I can, Ai-weh-deh." She took Gladys's hand and whispered again, "Go—take the children—the Japanese will soon be here. I learned they intend to kill you. God bless you and protect you and the children."

While they waited for Mrs. Cheng's brother, Gladys sat on a rock. She talked with the children.

"We've had little to eat," one said. "I've talked to the people in the village. Everyone who can is fleeing. They say, 'Get out while you can.' "

Ninepence added, "And Sualan tells us of terrible things that happen to girls when the Japanese soldiers come."

"Who is Sualan?" Gladys asked.

Ninepence pushed a rather large Chinese girl forward. "She's an escaped slave girl who was here in the caves when we came. Say she can join us, please! I love her so."

"Sualan." Gladys held out her hand. "You are joining a dangerous expedition. It is plain we must flee south with all these children. Are you willing to help carry the little ones, endure hardships?"

"Oh, yes, Ai-weh-deh. I'm used to heavy burdens."

"Welcome then. You bring our number to

GUESS	1. six hundred."
	2. one hundred."
	3. fifty."

"One hundred." Gladys shuddered at the responsibility.
"I'll see the

GUESS	1. governor."
	2. king."
	3. mandarin."

Gladys said, "I understand the mandarin is still here in Cheng Tsuen. But there is another problem. It is cold at night. Not as cold as a three-coat winter, but much too cold for these little ones to sleep outside."

"We'll snuggle close together and cuddle the small ones." The children nodded to each other. "And we can each carry a small comforter."

"Then you agree we should go?" Gladys asked.
"We

```
+----------+    1.  agree."
|  GUESS   |    2.  disagree."
+----------+    3.  are too afraid."
```

"We agree," they said.

Gladys found the mayor's house. He wore a plain blue robe and black skull cap. "What can I do for you?" The mandarin motioned Gladys to sit down.

"You can help me. I'm about to take one hundred children, aged three to sixteen, across the mountains to Shensi and safety."

"Why, you can't do that! That is miles and miles away. You have no food, no money. The little ones can never walk that far."

"The Lord will provide," Gladys said stubbornly.

"I'm not one to say He will *not* provide. I admire your spirit —but this *is foolish!*"

"Then you won't help?"

"Yes, I'll give you enough food for two days and send two men with you to carry it. But what is that out of so many days?"

"Thank you. You see, God has already supplied enough to start. Do you not think He can provide the rest?"

The mayor opened his mouth. He looked at Gladys in her quilted jacket and pants. He saw her determination. Then he closed his mouth without saying a word.

Early the next morning Gladys and the children started.

"Which way shall we go?" someone asked. "The Japanese are on every road."

"We won't take the roads. If we can find a mule track, we'll take that. Otherwise we just walk over the land and through the woods. We watch the sun, so we go in the right direction." Gladys spoke with more confidence than she felt.

At first the children

```
+----------+    1.  dawdled.
|  GUESS   |    2.  flew.
+----------+    3.  rode donkeys.
```

The children played and dawdled at first, but before nightfall they trudged quietly on sore feet. Older children finally carried the small ones on their backs.

At each village Gladys let the children rest while she

GUESS	1. took a swim. 2. begged for food. 3. played tennis.

When Gladys begged them for food, the people of most villages gave a two-day supply.

At night they slept

GUESS	1. by the roadside. 2. in temples. 3. in soldiers' camps.

Once they slept in a soldiers' camp, but usually they found a temple. If not, they huddled beside the path.

"Ai-weh-deh, my feet hurt!"

"Ai-weh-deh, my shoes are worn clean through!"

"Ai-weh-deh, my tummy aches."

"Ai-weh-deh, I can't go anymore."

"Ai-weh-deh, my back breaks."

"Ai-weh-deh, I'm not able to carry the little one any longer."

Gladys shortened the marches. She led in singing every hymn she knew. She started a Bible verse, and the children finished. They sang "Count Your Blessings" over and over.

Finally Ninepence objected. "We don't have any to count anymore. Sing something else."

After twelve weary days, they began asking each other,

GUESS	1. "How far to the Yellow River?" 2. "How many more days?" 3. "How many more mountains?"

91

Gladys wished she knew the answers to these questions. She told them, "When we get to the Yellow River, we will find a nice village called Yuen Chu. There we can find food, and you can swim in the river. We'll rest a little before we cross."

With this dream the children trudged on and on. Finally they topped a ridge and saw the

GUESS	1. village.
	2. river.
	3. desert.

"There it is! The river is yellow, truly yellow." The children broke their lines and ran toward the village.

"No one is here!" the children cried, going into every empty house. "There is no food."

"The people must have fled to the south, to Free China. Look in every kitchen." Gladys tried to sound convincing. "Some food must be left."

Finally she found a couple of Chinese soldiers. "Please give me some food for the children," she begged.

"How many you have?"

"One hundred."

"A hundred children? That's impossible. We have only a three-day supply of food ourselves. The Japanese will be here any day."

One soldier gave

GUESS	1. a carrot.
	2. a cabbage.
	3. a lamb.

Finally one soldier slipped Gladys a cabbage and two carrots. "Don't tell the others," he said.

Gladys found a kitchen where she boiled an enormous pot of water and added chopped cabbage and carrots. She found some nice looking leaves growing nearby and chopped them up, too. She sighed. "If the poor dears are hungry enough, they'll eat it."

She tried to sound cheerful. Everyone was too tired and disappointed to complain.

Next morning they were at the boat landing. "We'll catch the first boat going across the river this morning," she said, "and get food on the other side."

With six of the older boys, she went to military headquarters in town again.

"When are the boats going?"

"They're not. The ferry is closed. I told you we expect the Japanese any moment. They are overdue now."

Slowly Gladys walked to the boat landing with the boys. No one said anything, but Ninepence and Sualan knew by their faces there were no boats.

Gladys worried and fretted—then prayed. She watched the children playing in the water. Now and again one would come to her, and say, "Ai-weh-deh, I'm so hungry!"

"Oh, God, I'm at the end. I don't know what to do. I can't bear to see the children die. Not after they walked so far." Gladys prayed silently, *Help us, please.*

15

God's Power

Sualan tapped Gladys on her shoulder. "Ai-weh-deh, the others speak of Moses and the Red Sea. What do they mean? I, too, would like to know."

"Yes, yes, we will have a story. Come, children, gather round, and I'll tell you of other children, the *children of Israel*."

Gladys launched into one of her favorite stories. She told of the Israelites pouring out of Egypt. "They took their carrying poles, their wadded quilts, their shallow cooking pans. Just as we each carry chopsticks, a bowl, and a small wadded quilt, so the Israelites carried what they needed."

Gladys had lived in China so long she imagined she could see slant-eyed Israelites marching along. She finished the story by telling of Moses lifting his arms and the waves of the Red Sea parting as the people walked across on dry land. Everyone hushed for a moment.

Finally Sualan asked, "Why don't you hold up your arms and part the Yellow River so *we* can get across?"

"But I'm not Moses," Gladys objected. "That was a different time."

"And a different God?" Sualan asked.

"No, oh, no. He is the same God!" Gladys said. "And we must trust Him and ask for His power in our lives."

"Then why don't you hold up your hands and part the river?" Sualan persisted.

"Tell you what—let us all kneel and pray. Everyone pray as hard as you can." The children knelt. They thought she meant for them to pray aloud, and one hundred children cried out together, begging God's help.

After some time Gladys felt a tug on her jacket. She turned to a small boy. "Get up, get up! Big man here!"

Gladys stood up, trembling, before a large Chinese general.

"Are you in charge?"

"Yes," Gladys answered.

"How many children do you have?"

"One hundred."

"What are you doing here?" he questioned.

"Waiting to cross the Yellow River."

"But who are you?"

"I am Ai-weh-deh of Happiness Inn in Yangcheng."

"Are you crazy? The Japanese will attack if they see these children from the air. They will shoot them. It's strange they haven't come yet. Who are these children, anyway?"

"Refugees trying to reach Shensi."

"I'll signal for a boat." The general paused. "Insanity must be catching."

He whistled and raised his arm. "Boats will be across at once. You will find food on the other side if the Japanese planes don't gun you down."

"Thank you," Gladys said to the Chinese general's back. He walked away, shaking his head and muttering, "I'm as crazy as she is."

Back and forth the boats went until all the children were across. Gladys, Sualan, and Ninepence were in the last boatload. "We prayed to walk across like the children of Israel, but God knew we were too tired to walk. He sent us a boat. That's much better," Ninepence said.

Tears flowing down her cheeks, Gladys hugged each one.

"Oh, God . . . I don't know what to do."

At the village the children

GUESS

1. feasted.
2. received new shoes.
3. ran away.

The people of the village fed and even clothed some of the children.

Next day they sent them on their way to Mienchin with a two-day supply of food.

After eight more days of walking, the weary flock reached Mienchin. Gladys marched them to the train station.

"You think we are taking that crowd to the border of Free China—without money, without tickets?" the agent stared at Gladys in disbelief. "You'll have to talk to the master."

In a few minutes he returned with the stationmaster.

"You see, Sir," Gladys in her worn and dirty padded suit explained, "God has protected us for twenty days as we walked over the mountains. He even brought us over the Yellow River."

"And now you think *He* is sending you by *my* train?" The master looked stern.

"Can't you see, Sir, that these small children can walk no further? Look at their shoes worn through. Look at their faces. How many more days do you think they can survive?"

The stationmaster looked at Gladys. Cotton padding was showing through holes and rips in her suit. She was filthy, but hope showed in her eyes.

"Put them aboard!" the master commanded. "But remember, we do not cross the border. You will still have to walk the rest of the way."

Since most of the children had never seen a train, they were

GUESS

1. delighted.
2. angry.
3. fearful.

All loved to ride. "So much better than walking."
As the children watched from the windows, they saw

GUESS	1. mountains.
	2. flatlands.
	3. skyscrapers.

As the mountains disappeared, flatlands took their place.

"How many days would it take to walk all this way?" Ninepence wondered.

"I could do it in six days!" a boy bragged.

"Never—never!" Ninepence shoved him. "Such a smarty you think yourself."

At nightfall the train stopped. "End of the line!" the porters called. "All off!"

"But please, let the children sleep!" Gladys implored.

"No! We go back. The Japanese shoot at us if we stay too long."

So Gladys roused the older children and stepped onto the cold dark train platform. Stronger children carried sleeping ones and laid them on the rough planks.

"Stay here," Gladys directed Ninepence and the other older children.

Gladys hurried to a small fire, around which a few guards were gathered.

"We are on our way to the orphanage. Already we have walked twenty days. What can we do now?" she asked.

The guards looked at each other. One slowly spoke, "If I help, are you willing to obey?"

"Yes, if the children can get across the border."

"Are you willing to risk their lives?'

"Yes."

"Then I tell you. One train does go through. It is a coal train to Hua Shan. Sometimes the Japanese shoot at it and sometimes not. But if they see anyone, or hear voices, then they will shoot. Can you keep a hundred children quiet?"

The train left at 4:00 A.M. Carefully the stronger children placed the sleeping ones between large lumps of coal. "If you value your lives, keep your heads down," Gladys warned.

"And you, what about you?" Ninepence worried. "You carry children all day, you eat nothing yourself. You are ill!"

"I'll sleep lying between the coal chunks. We are all exhausted. I think everyone will sleep." Gladys prayed that she told the truth.

The train rolled quietly through the darkness. The little ones

GUESS	1. slept.
	2. cried.
	3. screamed.

Without a sound, the little ones slept.

Finally out of danger, the train reached its destination. When the children awoke, they screamed, "We turned black over night." They jumped around and wrestled with each other.

"They are as lively as crickets," Gladys marveled. "It is just as well, for I understand it is a three-day walk to Shensi."

The three-day walk took one hundred children

GUESS	1. four days.
	2. three days.
	3. six days.

After six days they reached the city and found a gate in the wall surrounding it.

"You cannot come in," the guards said. "No more refugees. We have no food—nothing—go away."

"But we walked twenty-seven days to get here," Gladys begged. She limped to the wall and sank down, leaning against it and staring speechless into space.

"If it's the orphanage you want," someone told her, "it is not inside the city anyway. It is in Fu-Feng."

Gladys was in such a daze she hardly knew how they finally reached the orphanage. She did know they walked without food, with little water, and under the hot sun for another day.

"This not like cool mountains," Ninepence said. "You look ill. Don't faint, little mother."

Gladys rubbed her black face, smearing the coal dust and sweat together. Under her padded suit, the sweat mixed with the coal dust. Gladys sweltered in the heat. She heard the children cry out, "Oh, there it is. See the sign 'Orphans Welcome'?"

Workers from the New Life Movement, begun by Madame Chiang Kai-shek, welcomed the children as they limped up the steps of the orphanage. "Oh," they cried, "they are half dead and so dirty."

Gladys refused to stay. She was ill, and her mind was confused. "I must go . . . hold meetings," she mumbled as she wandered. Finally she fell while trying to preach in a village.

16
Orchids

"But who is she?" the American missionaries asked.

"We don't know. We found her beside the road—fainted, drunk, or ill," three Chinese women explained.

"Why did you bring her here?"

"We found this in a pocket of her skirt."

The women held up a

GUESS	1. dollar. 2. Bible. 3. statue of Buddha.

"See this Bible with the funny writing. Looks English," the women said.

"It does indeed. Bring the poor soul inside," Dr. Hamilton, head of the mission, ordered. "I've never seen such a dirty person. She's covered with wet coal dust."

The Americans took Gladys to the

GUESS

1. airport.
2. hospital.
3. army camp.

In the hospital, Dr. Handley Stockly examined Gladys. "There is little hope. She has pneumonia and typhus. Who is she?" He looked puzzled. "She is suffering from malnutrition, exhaustion, and fever. She should have been dead long ago."

Gladys lay unconscious for

GUESS

1. six months.
2. one month.
3. ten months.

After a month Gladys had a visitor. She opened her eyes and said, "Mr. Lu!" Then she lapsed into a coma again.

"She is Ai-weh-deh of Happiness Inn," Mr. Lu explained.

Gladys

GUESS

1. died.
2. recovered.
3. never moved again.

Gladys recovered and began her work in Free China. She worked with

GUESS

1. refugees from North China.
2. lepers.
3. prisoners.

Gladys worked with all three groups, but her main job was to teach English at the University of Chuloo. One class consisted of Chinese officials. Most classes, however, were for college students.

102

"We love her," one student said. "She talks about God as though she knows Him."

Often she visited Ninepence and the other children in the orphanage nearby.

After

GUESS	1. five years
	2. seven years
	3. twenty years

Gladys realized the Communists were taking over all of China. It took seven years before Gladys could believe the Communists were really victorious. "I feel it is time to go home," she decided.

One day after class a student handed her an envelope. As Gladys opened it, all the pupils gathered around her. Inside she found

GUESS	1. money.
	2. a ticket.
	3. a note.

"A ticket to London on an airplane!" Gladys gasped. "Oh, my friends, how could you do it?"

"We

GUESS	1. gave money."
	2. sold things."
	3. stole it."

"We sold our clothes, shoes, and books. We gave all the money we had," the students explained.

Gladys hugged them all. Her body shook with joy and appreciation.

Two of the students walked with her to the airport—the only two college students who still had shoes.

In London the first familiar face she saw was that of

103

GUESS

1. Violet.
2. Mother.
3. Father.

Gladys's heart beat wildly when she saw Mother's face, then Father, then Violet, the twins, and Laurie. All were at the airport. All so much older. "How you've changed!" she exclaimed.

"Not as much as you!" they cried, pinning an orchid on her coat.

"Well, I'm almost forty-five. I would have called myself an old woman when I left London, but let's get home and catch up on the news. I want to know everything!"

Gladys didn't get much rest, however, because

GUESS

1. she starred in a movie.
2. she visited the queen.
3. she spoke in churches.

"I can't believe all these churches are asking me to tell my story." Gladys threw up her hands when she saw the pile of letters. "And would you believe, they always pin orchids on my suit before I speak? I do love the flower so much."

"We are proud of you." Father smiled. "But then we've always been proud of you, even when we called you 'Dumb Eyes.' "

"Oh, I finally learned I could read if I used a magnifying glass."

"You must have

GUESS

1. a new dress."
2. glasses."
3. a new hat."

"You must get glasses," Father insisted. "I'll pay for them myself. Too bad we didn't know about them when you were a child."

"Thank you, Father." Gladys patted his wrinkled old hand. "Don't take the money from your pension. The churches take up an offering every time I speak. I've never had so much money."

"What are you doing with it? You spend so little."

"I'm saving it to go back to China as soon as the war's over."

"Promise you'll stay with me as long as I live," Mother begged with tears in her eyes. "I can't bear to lose you again."

Gladys looked into her mother's eyes for long moments. She said,

GUESS	1. "I can't promise that."
	2. "Wait and see."
	3. "Very well."

Seeing the frail, withered body of her mother, Gladys promised to stay.

Seven years later Gladys got a call on the new telephone she had put in her parents' home.

"This is Alan Burgess of New York. I heard of your story and would like to write a book, telling the world of your adventures."

Gladys gasped. "About me? Why I'm just an ordinary, uneducated person. There's nothing to write about me."

"That's not true. I want to come to London. We can sit down, and you can tell me everything. It would really be *you* telling the story. Say yes, please. We'd pay you."

Gladys said,

GUESS	1. "No."
	2. "Yes."
	3. "I don't know."

"You know, it would be a way to let people know of God's leading and His protection. It might help someone answer God's call. Yes, I'll do it!"

E. P. Dutton published the book in 1957. Alan Burgess named it

| GUESS |

1. *God's Glory.*
2. *The Small Woman.*
3. *China.*

The Small Woman was so successful that Gladys's story was made into a movie.

Gladys could not go back to Communist China, but she could go to Formosa (called Taiwan today). When Gladys's plane touched down in Taiwan, she began her search for

| GUESS |

1. needy children.
2. a location for the orphanage.
3. Madame Chiang Kai-shek.

Madame Chiang Kai-shek met her plane. "Thank you, dear, for working with the children of China," she said. "Please come with me."

Together they went to a waiting automobile. On the way Madame Chiang explained, "I have cried many tears for China. We did what we could to keep the Communists out, but they told the people lies, and we were forced to flee to this island."

"And the children? What of them?"

"We brought them along, but now they are scattered. Many have grown up and work in Hong Kong or wherever they can find employment."

When the automobile stopped, Madame Chiang said good-bye. Gladys stepped out and was swept off her feet by

| GUESS |

1. the mandarin.
2. Ninepence.
3. the general.

"Ninepence, oh, Ninepence!" Gladys wept. "How lovely you are!"

"God has been good to me. I have a good husband and a child. We expect you to live with us here. Come inside the mission and see some of the others."

Gladys lived with Ninepence and her husband while she organized a refugee mission in Hong Kong and an orphanage near Tayseh. She loved the couple so much that she left Ninepence's husband in charge while she traveled to raise money for the work.

Gladys traveled to

GUESS	1. Germany.
	2. England.
	3. the United States.

Christians in the United States begged her to come in 1959. "Tell us of China. Tell us how God protected you and the children on your journey to safety." Everywhere she was welcomed with orchids. Americans opened their hearts to the small woman.

When Gladys returned to Taiwan, she

GUESS	1. opened more camps.
	2. started more orphanages.
	3. led a revolt.

Gladys started more orphanages because homeless children still roamed the streets, eating from garbage cans and sleeping in alleys. The American organization World Vision helped her.

One orphanage was in Taiwan, where Gladys found a peaceful home. *It's been thirty years since I left the London train station. God has at last given me a peaceful place to work, wonderful people to help me, and blessed children. Nothing more could happen to me now,* she thought.

Gladys was shocked when she received a telegram from the British broadcasting station. "You have a ticket to London and back waiting for you at the airport. Come at once!"

Fear filled her heart as she stepped off the plane in London on March 28, 1963. She told the taxi driver, "Take me to the British broadcasting TV station. Please hurry!"

When she entered the studio, she saw a sign, "This Is Your Life." She was seated like a queen, as the narrator told the television audience about her life. Violet came to the platform, then Laurie, her brother. Her heart missed a few beats when Mr. Lu came in. Dr. Handley Stockly, who had saved her life in Free China, appeared.

The moderator asked her a few questions. "In your childhood did you have any idea you would do great things for God?"

"No. When I was a child, the children said I was dumb. But Mother said God made me for a purpose, and He would use me if I was willing."

"Why did you go to China with no sponsor or money?"

Gladys became thoughtful. "You know, I don't think I was God's first choice for what I've done in China. There was somebody else, a man perhaps. But for some reason he wouldn't go. He wouldn't answer God's call. Anyway, God looked down and saw me and said, 'Well, at least she's willing!' "

A few weeks later Gladys went back to her orphanage in Taiwan and served faithfully until she died on January 4, 1970. She was sixty-eight years old.

Moody Press, a ministry of the Moody Bible Institute, is designed for education, evangelization, and edification. If we may assist you in knowing more about Christ and the Christian life, please write us without obligation: Moody Press, c/o MLM, Chicago, Illinois 60610.